PARSLEY, SAGE, ROSEMARY AND MINE

an herbal faire

of

susan a. mccreary

"herbs virtues are that they give an uncommon warmth and vigor to the blood and frisks the spirits beyond any other cordial, they cheer the heart even of a man that has a bad wife."

william byrd

a strawberry patchworks book

11597 southington lane
herndon, virginia
22070

© copyright susan a. mccreary 1991

to the five most important people in my life:

Estelle -   my mother who taught me all I know about herbs and the good life.
Robert -   my husband who has shown me the good life and allowed me to grow.
Mallory -   my daughter who loves good food and who keeps me in the 20th Century.
Rob -   my son who endured test recipes and keeps the fun in this journey of life.
Tom -   my brother who makes me proud of this family & is the true gourmand.

SPECIAL THANKS TO CATHY ALIFRANGIS:
She was my editor, my arbiter of appropriateness, my technical assistant, my recipe tester, my friend.

Library of Congress Cataloging-in-Publication Data

mccreary, susan a. (susan abernathy)
parsley, sage, rosemary, and mine: an herbal faire

p. cm.
ISBN 0-9608428-5-3
1. Cookery (herbs) 2. Herbs. 3. Herbs-Folklore. I. Title.
TX819.H4M4 1991
641.6'57--dc20   91-37719
                CIP

an herbal banquet

a stillroom of gifts 7

a tisane of drinks 15

a sampler of appetizers 27

a knot garden of salads 43

a simple of soups 59

a wreath of breads 71

a potpourri of entrees 83

a tussie mussie of vegetables 105

a topiary of desserts and pies 121

a pomander of cakes and cookies 141

A TRIBUTE TO THE WITCH DOCTOR

This book is about memories all centering around herbs. This delves into the past, my past and my life with "an herb". The inspiration comes from her - it was to be her book. She wrote countless articles, spiced up many bland meals and still touches many lives. She healed many a child's warts with her suggestible "wart oil". When she passed around her beauty herbs at herb lectures, there were those dowagers who surreptiously dabbed a drop on their turkey necks. She was "The Witch Doctor;" her very self was a balm to weary souls. Today she still dispenses forklore to the unsuspecting, while comforting those with the vapours.

Of course she created a family rich in all the good properties of herbs. Mine was a life inextricably intertwined with herbs. Her herb kitchen, her still room, her soul room was an enchanted retreat. I longed to know what secrets those jars held, and as a child, would sit in the herb kitchen and try to absorb the ages. Estelle Abernathy, the noted herbalist, taught me about the wonder of herbs.

This is a cookbook with some of the excitement of herbs strewn about the pages. With this book, you will find seasoning with herbs far more healthful than using salt. Never be afraid to use herbs in anything. Daddy said Mother used garlic in all but fudge & coffee. Try it.

This is a book to continue your herbal quest with some favorite foods. This is a book of my rememberances of going to Scarborough Fair. But most of all, this is a tribute to her and the magic she, as well as herbs, brought into my life.

FORWARD

*Oh, where are you going? To Scarborough Fair.
Savory, sage, rosemary and thyme,
Remember me to a lass who lives there,
For once she was a true love of mine.*

Those are words from the "task song" that Simon & Garfunkle slightly changed for their popular song. But the song has that theme of remembrances that so often characterizes herbs & herbal lore.

A few notes about the herbs in our title - parsley, sage, rosemary and thyme.

Parsley: Mother said to many a startled diner "You would be better off to eat the parsley and leave the main course." Packed with calcium, thiamin, riboflavin & niacin, Vitamins A & C and a great breath purifier, it is nonetheless said "only the wicked can grow parsley." When sown, it is notoriously slow to germinate because it goes to the devil seven times before coming up. It was a sacred herb to the Greeks and as such could not be brought to the table. Perhaps we love it so because the country saying "Where parsley flourishes, Missus is Master" shows our cultivating skills.

Sage: the herb one embraces in midlife. The saying "Why should a man die while sage grows in his garden?" Sir John Hill wrote "Sage will retard the rapid progress of decay that treads upon our heels so fast in the latter years of life, will prolong the faculties & memory...." Perhaps we should wear sage bonnets.

Rosemary: that holy plant so entwined with Christian legends and turning away evil but equally promoted as the herb of friendship & remembrance.

The herbalist, Gerard, said "Rosemary, if a garland there be put about the head it comforteth the brain...and the heart and make it merry." Shakespeare said to smell of it oft and it shall keep you youngly.

Thyme: the herb of courage, energy & activity. It is associated with bees and in medieval days, a maiden often would embroider a scarf for a knight to wear in battle with a bee hovering over a sprig of thyme. It is said the odor is so healing, Hippocrates rubbed oil of thyme on his forehead for headaches & fainting spells. Thyme was worn by young girls hoping to find sweethearts. It was the manger herb and is always included in the manger scene - perhaps for the aroma and the healing.

There are countless herbs with equally efficacious properties. Marjoram was tucked in hope chests to help find a husband. Then it was used to polish the furniture. Mint was used to keep ladies from swooning. The ancient Hebrews scattered mint on synagogue floors. Each footstep wafted fragrance. Violets can be bound about the head and sleep would overtake one immediately. Mandrake keeps evil spirits from harming a sleeping family. There are herbs to cure baldness, toothaches & poverty. Try these recipes, you could discover a delightful side effect!

Enjoy this trip back in time, to a time of Scarborough Fair with modern conveniences and prepared foods. Experience the wonder, the excitement, the surprises of using herbs.....and remember.

a stillroom of gifts

*The Abernathy Herb Kitchen
Newport News, Virginia*

Mother' herb kitchen was her stillroom
Great concoctions happened there;
A wart was vanished; a dimple poked,
There was magic in that air.

Witches brew simmering over a fire,
Cutting cookies over a trestle;
Mixing herb blends or curing the vapors
Amonst a family of mortar & pestles.

HERBAL JELLY

For all jellies use:
3½ C sugar   3 oz pectin

For all herbal jellies, make an herbal infusion by mixing chopped herbs with ¼ C sugar (4 T dried herbs may be used for 1 C fresh). Place in a heavy 4 qt pan. Stir in the required liquids & bring to a boil. Simmer 8 minutes & bring to a rolling boil; stir in pectin; boil ½ minute, stirring constantly. Add remaining sugar & bring to a full boil that cannot be stirred down. Boil 1 minute. Remove from heat & skim off foam. Pour through a sieve into prepared jars & seal.

BASIL JELLY
1 C tomato juice   2 T basil
¼ C lemon juice   ¼ C water

LEMON THYME JELLY
1½ T lemon thyme   ½ C water
         1 C red wine

PURPLE BASIL & ORANGE JELLY
1½ C purple basil   ½ C wine vinegar
1⅔ C orange juice   6 whole cloves
      zest of 1 orange (no white)

RED ROSEMARY JELLY
2 oranges, sliced   2 C cranberries
½ C rosemary   5 whole cloves

PARSLEY JELLY
3 bunches parsley   1 lemon, juiced

MINT JULEP JELLY

2 C mint ½ C whiskey
½ C sherry

CINNAMON WINE JELLY

2 C port ½ t grn cinnamon
5 1½" sticks cinnamon

SAGE JELLY

1 T sage ¼ C water
1 ¼ C red wine

HORSERADISH JELLY

¼ C prepared horseradish ¼ C vinegar

FRESH GINGER JELLY

¼ lb gingerroot 1 C water
6 T lemon juice

SWEET MARJORAM JELLY

2 T marjoram ¼ C lime juice
1 C pineapple juice ¼ C water

HERBAL VINEGARS

Any fruit, herb, seed, flower or spice can be used to flavor warm vinegar. Let steep for 2 weeks. Use white wine vinegar for delicate herbs & cider vinegar with strong herbs. Never let vinegar boil.

VINEGAR OF THE FOUR THIEVES

2 qt cider vinegar	2 T rue
2 T lavender	2 T wormwood
2 T rosemary	2 T mint
2 T minced garlic	2 T sage

SPICED VINEGAR

2 C wine vinegar	6 whole cloves
1 t whole allspice	1 bay leaf
1 t coriander seeds	2 T sugar
1 t shelled cardamon seed	1 cinnamon stick

gifts

PUMPKIN CHIP MARMALADE

6 lb sliced pumpkin rind   1 oz gingerroot
8 oz candied ginger   6 lbs sugar
1 T ground ginger   3 sliced lemons

Chop all coarsely & boil until pumpkin is clear in color. Put in jars & seal.

GARLIC JAM

2½ C chopped garlic cloves   ¾ C sugar
                 ¼ C water

Boil all over high heat, stirring constantly & simmer until garlic is soft & golden, about 25 minutes. Chill covered.

CRANBERRY MARMALADE

1 large gingerroot   4 C water
2 lbs cranberries   4 C sugar

Chop gingerroot fine & boil all together stirring constantly. Simmer for 1 hour & skim the foam from the top. Seal in jars.

BASIL PESTO

2 C basil leaves   ½ t pepper
3 cloves garlic   ½ C olive oil
2 T parsley   3 T pine nuts
½ C parmesan cheese   salt to taste

Combine all ingredients in a processor. Puree until a smooth paste. Keep refrigerated. Can be frozen.

Keep some rosemary leaves in a jar of sugar to use in tea or desserts.

APRICOT ORANGE CHUTNEY

¾ C chopped apricots   ½ C diced apples
¾ C water   1 T minced onion
¾ C honey   2 T lemon juice
¼ C chopped walnuts   3 drops Tabasco
½ C orange pulp   ¼ t grn cinnamon
⅛ t grtd nutmeg   ¼ C coconut
        ½ t grated orange rind

Combine apricots, water & honey in a pan & bring to a boil. Reduce heat & simmer until water is absorbed, stirring often. Cool & mix with other ingredients. Let stand 1 hour before serving. Makes 1½ C.

GINGERED PEACH CHUTNEY

¼ C lime juice   ¾ C apple jelly
2 T chopped gingerroot   1 chopped onion
1 chopped seeded jalapeño 1½ T vinegar
        2½ lbs peaches, chopped

Cook juice, ginger, pepper, jelly & onion over low heat, covered until onion is tender (6-8 minutes). Bring to a boil & add peaches & vinegar. Cook 7 minutes. Seal or refrigerate. Makes 3 cups.

Flavor brandy with any herbs to use for flambe or sauces. 1 C herbs = 2 C brandy.

Garlic is the catsup of intellectuals.

MINT CHUTNEY

6 C vinegar	½ lb raisins
2 lbs brown sugar	4 apples
1 oz mustard seed	2 onions
2 C mint leaves	1 t red pepper
4 green tomatoes	3 oz salt

Boil vinegar & sugar together until dissolved. Remove from heat. Chop the fruits & vegetables & add to vinegar with salt. Let stand 2 days, stirring some. Use on meats.

ITALIAN HERB SEASONING

This can be your all purpose seasoning. Use on eggs, salads, meats etc. in place of salt.

½ t cayenne pepper	1 t thyme
1 T garlic powder	1 t savory
1 t basil	1 T parsley
1 t onion powder	1 t sage
1 t black pepper	1 t marjoram

Mix all ingredients until blended. Store in airtight container.

SPICY CRANBERRY RELISH

1 lb cranberry sauce	¼ t cinnamon
¼ t mace or nutmeg	¼ t dry mustard
½ C drained, crushed pineapple	

Mix all ingredients until blended. Chill for at least 1 hour for flavors to blend. Makes 1 pint.

Herb Flour makes nice gifts; use on meats

2 C flour	½ t salt
1-2 t minced dried herbs	4 turns peppermill

gifts

FRESH MINT RELISH

1 ½ C cider vinegar
1 C sugar
2 t dry mustard
½ C chopped onions

1 ¼ C apple
1 tomato
½ C raisins
¼ t salt

3 T chopped mint

Scald the vinegar. Add sugar & mustard. Cool. Combine all ingredients in a processor & blend. Seal in a quart jar.

HOT & SPICY BANANA KETCHUP

1 C raisins
1 C chopped onion
3 cloves garlic
6 oz tomato paste
2⅔ C vinegar
8 large bananas
4 C water
1 C brown sugar

1 T salt
1 t cayenne
½ C corn syrup
4 t grn allspice
1 ½ t cinnamon
1 ½ t grt nutmeg
1 t pepper
½ t cloves

¼ C dark rum

Combine first 10 ingredients in a processor. Puree until smooth. Put in a pan & boil over medium heat, stirring frequently. Turn heat to low & simmer uncovered for 1 ¼ hours. If mixture gets too thick, add more water. Then add syrup & spices & cook 15 minutes more. Remove from heat. Thin with vinegar & water if necessary. Combine all ingredients in a processor. Return to heat & add rum. Ladle into jars. Makes 7 cups.
Variation: Substitute 4 strips orange zest, 8 C cranberries & 1 t ground ginger for the raisins, tomato paste, bananas & cayenne. Cook as directed.

PINEAPPLE PICKLE

40 oz pineapple chunks
1½ C white vinegar
2½ C sugar
dash of salt
2 cinnamon stks
15 whole cloves

Bring the pineapple juice, vinegar, sugar & spices to a boil. Add pineapple chunks & boil again. Remove from heat & store covered in the refrigerator until needed. Serves 10.

GARLIC PICKLES

1 gal sour pickles
1 whole head of garlic
5 lbs sugar
1 bx pickling spice

Drain vinegar from pickles & slice in ½" slices. Layer the pickles, garlic cloves, sugar & pickling spice in a jar. Marinate for 2 weeks.

DILLED MUSTARD

½ C dry mustard
½ C vinegar
6 T sugar
2 T water
1 t salt
1 T dill
1 beaten egg

Mix all ingredients except egg & let stand at room temperature for ½ a day. Add egg & cook on low until thick, about 8 minutes. Keep in a jar in refrigerator. Serve with corned beef or ham.

Mustard's no good without roast beef!
Chico Marx

a tisane of drinks

Libations for morning, noon or night;
Infusions for the weary of heart;
A pot of herb tea, her cherry bounce,
And always a story to start.

drinks

CANCUN CANTALOPE FROST

1 C cantaloupe squares   ¼ ground ginger
1 C cold milk   2 C orange sherbet

Freeze cantaloupe cubes until firm. When firm process with milk and ginger until slushy. Add the sherbet a spoonful at a time until thoroughly mixed. Serve in chilled shallow glasses. Serves 4.

ALOHA JULIUS

½ C cream of coconut   1 ½ C orange juice
½ t ginger   1 C vanilla ice cream

Mix all ingredients in a blender or processor. Add crushed ice & blend. Serves 4.

FIESTA COCONUT CONCOCTION

1 C coconut ice cream   1 banana, cubed
½ C orange juice concentrate   ¼ C mint leaves
   ¾ C milk
8 ¼ oz crushed pineapple   4 ice cubes

Mix the ice cream, orange juice, pineapple and its juice, banana, mint and milk in a processor until blended. Add the ice, one cube at a time until thickened. Serve chilled at once with mint sprigs as garnish. Serves 6.

Herbs are considered to be the leaves, roots & stems of the plant while spices are the seeds of the plant.

FROSTY MINT DRINK

1 C sugar
1 C water
16 6" mint stalks
1 C lemon juice
1 C grapefruit juice
ginger ale

Make a simple syrup by boiling sugar & water together for 5 minutes. Pour over mint, cover & steep for 5 minutes. Drain, squeezing the mint to capture the mint essence. Add juices & chill. When serving pour mixture into half a glass; fill glass with ice & ginger ale. Serves 6-8.

ROSEMARY LEMONADE

3 t rosemary
½ C honey
4 C water
⅔ C lemon juice

Simmer the chopped rosemary with honey and 1 C water for 5 minutes. Strain out rosemary and add hot liquid to the rest of the water and lemon juice. Chill & serve with a lemon slice. Serves 1.

APPLESAUCE SLUSH

This is good enough for a drink or dessert!

2 C applesauce
¼ C raspberry preserves
1 t cinnamon
¾ C yogurt
½ t vanilla
raspberries

Mix applesauce, preserves and cinnamon and freeze in a shallow pan until firm. Place in a processor with yogurt and vanilla & blend until smooth. Pour into glasses & garnish with raspberries. Serves 4.

drinks

CITRUS SODA

8 oz soda water	1 orange
1 C grapefruit juice	½ C orange sherbet
½ C pineapple juice	Mint leaves

Combine soda water, and juices. Section & peel orange and divide among 4 glasses. Pour soda mix evenly into glasses. Top with 2 T sherbet & garnish with mint leaves. Serves 4.

BLACKBERRY CORDIAL

An excellent check for slight dysentery!

1 pt. blackberry juice	¼ oz mace
1 lb sugar	2 T cloves
½ oz cinnamon	1 C brandy

Mash warm blackberries to extract juice. Boil all except brandy together for 15 minutes; strain; and to each pint add 1 C brandy.

Variation: Substitute 1 oz of mint leaves and 2½ C water for the blackberry juice and spices.

KICKY GRAPE JUICE

2 C grape juice	1⅔ C water
2 T sugar	1 t cinnamon
2 T lemon juice	pinch of ginger

Mix all ingredients in a pan & cook until hot. Serve hot or cold. Makes 4 cups.

PEACH FIZZ

A delightful daiquiri type drink.

6 oz vodka or rum   3 oz water
3 peeled peaches   ½ C mint
    16 oz can lemonade concentrate

Blend all ingredients in a blender until smooth. Combine in blender with ice until frothy. Garnish with mint. Serves 4.

Add these herbs to a pint of madeira:
1 sprig wormwood and rosemary
1 small bruised nutmeg
1 inch ginger root & cinnamon bark

Steep for a week in a dark, cool room & add to a fresh pint of madeira.

POTPOURRI TEA

1 t dried roses   ⅛ t cloves
1 t strawberry leaves   1 C hot water
¼ t cinnamon   1 t lemon juice

Place roses, leaves & spices in a glass jar and add water no warmer than 180°. Add lemon juice & steep 5-10 minutes. Sweeten with honey if desired. Serves 1.

"Love and scandal are the best sweeteners of tea"
                             Henry Fielding

drinks

CRANBERRY TEA

2 C cranberry juice　　¼ t salt
20 oz pineapple juice　½ t whole allspice
½ C brown sugar　　　1 T whole cloves
2 C water　　　　　　3 cinnamon sticks

Mix juices, sugar, water, salt and add spices. Simmer until ready to use. Serves 6.

HOT BIRD

¾ oz creme de cacao　2 t milk
1½ oz tequila　　　　Hot water
2 dashes allspice　　Whipped cream
　　　ground nutmeg garnish

Mix the liquors, allspice, & milk in a mug. Fill with hot water & garnish with whipped cream & nutmeg. Serves 1.

GINGER TEA

Pound 3 slices of ginger root with a hammer. Add 2 C boiling water & steep for 2 hours. Add lemon juice & honey.

CIDER SPICE BALL

Mix ⅓ C cinnamon chips, ⅓ C whole cloves, ⅓ C whole allspice, ⅔ C orange peel & oil.

MEXICAN HOT CHOCOLATE

2 C milk
1 C cream
½ t cinnamon
6 T sugar
1 egg
1 t vanilla
2 squares unsweetened chocolate

Heat the milk & cream on low until hot but not boiling. Add the cinnamon and sugar. Beat the egg and vanilla. Melt the chocolate and mix all together slowly. Heat on low until hot beating until frothy. Serves 4.

MINTED HOT CHOCOLATE

4 C scalded milk
4 T cocoa
¾ t vanilla
pinch of salt
10 mint leaves

Pour scalded milk over cocoa in a pot. Add vanilla & salt. Place 2 mint leaves in each cup & pour hot chocolate over. Serves 4.

SPIKED COFFEE

1 C strong coffee
1 slice lemon peel
½ cinnamon stick
1 allspice berry
1 clove
½ t rum extract
1 t sugar
1 oz vodka

Simmer the coffee and spices covered for 10 minutes. When ready to serve, add extract, sugar & vodka & heat. Serves 1.

drinks

CAFE HAWAII

1 qt cold coffee   4 C pineapple juice
1 qt vanilla ice cream   2 t ground ginger

Combine all ingredients & beat on low until smooth & frothy. Serve immediately to 8.

COFFEE MAGNOLIA

4 C cold coffee   1 qt chocolate or
½ C sugar   buttered almond
¼ t almond extract   ice cream

Mix coffee, sugar & extract. Soften ice cream & stir into coffee mixture. Serve in punch cups. Serves 12.

MOCHO COCOA MIX

1½ C dry milk powder   ½ C sugar
½ t ground cinnamon   ½ C cocoa
¼ t ground nutmeg   ⅛ t ground cloves
¼ C instant coffee   Brandy

Mix all the dry ingredients and store in an airtight jar. When ready to serve add 2 T mix to 1 Cup boiling water. Add a splash of brandy & whipped cream. Makes 22 cups.

Benedictine and Chartreuse were made with herbs, especially lemon balm, thought to insure longevity.

MINTY MOCHA MIX

2 hard peppermint candies
½ C powdered sugar
½ C powdered milk
¼ C instant coffee
2 T cocoa

In processor crush the candy finely. Add all else & store in an airtight jar. To serve mix 2 T mix to 1 C boiling water. Makes 1 cup.

TEA & COCOA SYMPATHY MIX

1 ¼ C instant tea powder with lemon & sugar
1 C cocoa
2 t cinnamon

Mix all together & store in an airtight container. Add 3 T mix to 1 C hot milk. Serves 20.

HERB TEAS

Combine herbs and water, bring to a boil and allow to simmer for 15 minutes. When using dried leaves use 1 tsp to 1 C boiling water; for fresh herbs use 3 to 4 times more than dried. When using seeds, crush with mortar & pestle. Use 1 heaping tsp to 1 C water. Use anise, caraway, dill, fennel, and coriander seeds. Use basil, mint, parsley, rosemary, marjoram, sage, savory and thyme leaves. Herb Teas are best sweetened with honey, sometimes lemon but never milk.

For those who love to be invalids, drink strong green tea, eat pickles, preserves and rich pastry.
        Lydia Childs 1829

drinks

SPICY PEACH PUNCH

46 oz peach nectar   *3 cinnamon stks*
2½ C orange juice   *½ t whl cloves*
½ C brown sugar   *2 T lime juice*

Mix peach nectar, orange juice & sugar in a pan. Add broken cinnamon sticks and cloves & simmer 10 minutes. Stir in lime juice. Serve hot in mugs to 10.

Variation: Substitute cranberry & apple juices for the peach & orange juices.

CINNAMON PUNCH

½ C sugar   *¼ C red hot*
46 oz pineapple   *cinnamon candies*
grapefruit juice drink   *1 qt ginger ale*

Heat sugar, juice drink and candies until dissolved. Chill; add ginger ale and crushed ice or freeze slushy. Serves 20.

MINT SPARKLE PUNCH

(This color should be patented!)

10 oz mint jelly   *½ C lemon juice*
2 C hot water   *12 oz gingerale*
    3 C pineapple juice

Combine jelly in hot water & stir until dissolved Add all else just before serving and pour over ice. Serves 10-12.

drinks
25

PUNCH FOR THIRSTY HORDES

1 C hot water
2 C mint leaves
1½ gal sweetened tea
92 oz pineapple juice
24 oz orange juice concentrate
24 oz lemonade
2 qts ginger ale

Pour hot water over mint & steep until cool. Remove mint and combine water, tea & juices. Add ginger ale just before serving in a punch bowl. Serves 100.

SPICED ICED TEA

2 qts boiling water
5 tea bags
2 cinnamon sticks
1½ C pineapple juice
1 C pickled peach juice
3 lemons & 3 oranges juiced
1½ C sugar
Mint leaves

Pour hot water over tea bags & broken cinnamon sticks & steep 30 minutes. Discard bags & cinnamon & add remaining ingredients including juice drained from spiced pickled peaches. Chill. Serves 12.

WAKE UP SHAKE UP

1 medium banana
1 C strawberries
1 T honey
¼ t nutmeg
1 C flavored yogurt

Process all ingredients until smooth, Serves 2.

Witches abhor dill so that they will not enter a house if a sprig be hung over the door.
Culpepper

drinks
26

ALMOND CREME LIQUEUR

14 oz condensed milk	4 eggs
1¾ C amaretto liqueur	2 t vanilla
2 t almond extract	1 C cream

1 t instant coffee powder

Mix all ingredients in a processor & blend well. Store in a closed jar in refrigerator for up to 1 month. Stir & serve chilled. Makes 4½ cups.

CHAMPAGNE PEACH CUP

2 Pkgs frozen peaches	1 C sugar
½ lemon, juiced	2 C ice
1 C boiling water	1 pt champagne
1 t ground ginger	fresh peaches

Whirl all ingredients except for fresh peaches in the blender. Pour into champagne flutes & garnish with fresh peach slices. Serve with demitasse spoons. Serves 6.

CHOCOHOLICS LIQUEUR

1½ C sugar	3 C vodka
5 T cocoa powder	1 vanilla bean,
¾ C water	split

Bring sugar, cocoa powder & water to a boil & simmer on low just until dissolved. Cool to room temperature. Stir in vodka & vanilla bean. Cover tight & store in a bottle of vodka for 1-2 weeks.

a sampler of appetizers

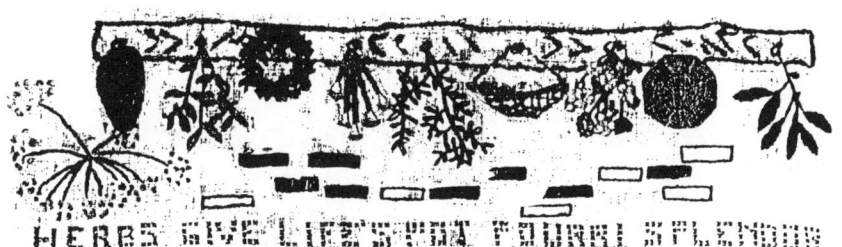

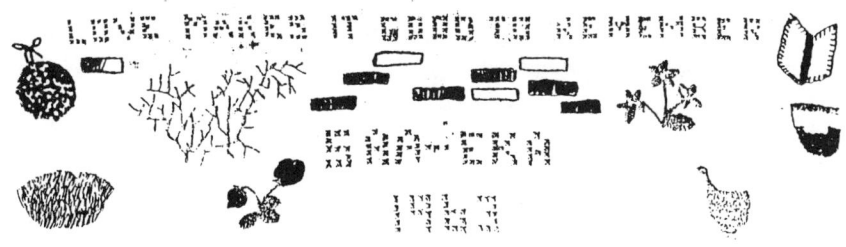

*Lovingly created to reflect an herb talk;
Stitched with herb dyed thread;
Reminding us of life's rich joys
On the herb strewn path we tread.*

appetizers

HONEST HERB DIP

1 C mayonnaise	1 garlic clove
½ t lemon juice	¼ t salt
½ t marjoram	½ t thyme
½ t worcestershire sauce	½ t parsley
⅛ t curry powder	¼ t paprika
1 T grated onion	¾ C sour cream

Mince all ingredients together in a processor. Serve with an assortment of fresh vegetables.

CHINESE GINGER JOY

1 C mayonnaise	1 C plain yogurt
¼ C dried onions	¼ C parsley
¼ C water chestnuts	2 cloves garlic
½ T candied ginger	1 T soy sauce

Chop all ingredients and mix well. Garnish with additional minced candied ginger. Make 2 days ahead to allow flavors to make joy.

HOT SPINACH ARTICHOKE DIP

10 oz chopped spinach	2 T minced onion
7 oz artichoke hearts	2 slices bacon
1 C cream	1 bouillon cube
¼ C Parmesan cheese	⅛ t season.salt
¼ t onion powder	tortilla chips

Thaw and drain spinach and artichoke hearts and chop. Add all except chips to a pan & bring to a boil. Simmer uncovered for 5 minutes, stirring. Serve warm with chips. Makes 2 cups.

appetizers
29

OLIVES OREGANO - TO EACH 1 LB OF PRICKED OLIVES IN A JAR, ADD 1 C OIL, 1 t THYME, 1 t CRUSHED PEPPERCORNS, 3 t OREGANO. MARINATE IN JAR FOR 3 DAYS.

PECAN PARSLEY DIP

2 C plain yogurt
1 garlic clove
1 small cucumber
¾ C toasted pecans
½ C parsley
½ t paprika
dash cayenne
pinch salt

Mix the yogurt with the minced garlic & chopped cucumber and pecans. Add the herbs and season to taste with the cayenne pepper. Salt may not be needed. Chill for at least 2 hours. Serve with crackers or vegetables.

MEXICAN HAT DANCE DIP

1 C cottage cheese
1 T diced onion
1 hard cooked egg white
2 t chili salsa
⅛ t paprika
½ t dry mustard
½ C buttermilk
1 T lemon juice
¼ C skim milk
tortilla chips

Combine all ingredients but the milk & chips in the processor, adding the milk a bit at a time until desired thickness is achieved. Blend until smooth. Sprinkle more paprika over top & serve with chips. Makes 1½ cups.

appetizers

HOT HERBED PRETZELS

1 C butter	1 t parsley
1 pkg pretzels	½ t tarragon
¼ t celery salt	¼ t onion salt

Melt butter, add pretzels & all else. Coat well. Heat at 400° 15 minutes. Makes 4 C.

GINGERED AVOCADO DIP

1 small avocado	½ C honey
¼ C lime juice	1 C plain yogurt
2 T chopped candied ginger	

Blend until smooth. Chill & use as a dip for fruit. Makes 2 cups.

MIDDLE EASTERN OLIVE SPREAD

2 C roasted peppers	2 t thyme
1 C pitted black olives	1 T vinegar
¼ C olive oil	2 T parsley
2 minced garlic cloves	½ t capers
1 t anchovy paste	black pepper

Chop the red or green peppers & olives & mix all together. Serve with crackers. Serves 8.

PEANUT BUTTER CHILI DIP

An unlikely delicious combination!

½ C chunky peanut butter	½ C chili sauce
1 T horseradish	1 T lemon juice

Stir all together; cover & chill. Serve with raw vegetables. Makes 1 cup.

appetizers
31

SHRIMP WITH A PARSLEY COLLAR

24 jumbo shrimp
3 oz cream cheese
1 oz roquefort cheese

½ t mustard
⅛ t garlic salt
1 C parsley

Cook shrimp in salted water until pink, 3-5 minutes. Drain, peel, split the vein side & chill. Blend cheeses, prepared mustard & garlic salt & with a pastry tube fill the split side with the cheese mix. Roll cheese side in chopped parsley.

SHRIMP MARINADE KABOB

1 lb medium shrimp
½ C olive oil
¼ C wine vinegar
2 T orange juice
2 t grated orange peel
1 minced garlic clove

½ t red pepper
¼ t black pepper
2 oranges, cubed
½ cucumber, cubed
18 stuffed green olives

Marinate shrimp in next 7 ingredients. Put shrimp on a pick with the remaining ingredients.

SCALLOPS WITH GREEN HERBS

1 lb scallops
¼ C any green herbs
¼ C parsley

¼ C onions
2 garlic cloves
½ C butter

Mix scallops with chopped up herbs, onions & garlic & cook in butter until tender. Serve on skewers.

appetizers
32

COCONUT SHRIMP

1 lb medium shrimp   1 C flour
1 qt oil   3½ oz coconut
12 oz soda water   Honey sauce

Peel shrimp leaving tails on. Heat oil to 350°. Make a batter with soda water & whisk in flour a bit at a time beating smooth. Place 2 dishes, one with additional flour & one with shredded coconut. Dip shrimp in flour, then in batter & coat with coconut. Fry in hot oil 1½ - 2 minutes until golden. Drain & serve with Honey Sauce.

HONEY SAUCE

Blend ⅓ cup each sour cream, honey, Dijon mustard & ¾ t cayenne pepper.

FUJIAMA SHRIMP

9 oz shrimp   French bread
1 T butter   1 T mustard
1 t Dijon mustard   ¼ C butter
¼ t chopped gingerroot   sliced scallions

Mix shrimp, 1 T butter, 1 t Dijon & chopped or grated gingerroot. Cut French bread into ¼" slices and spread with butter mixed with mustard. Spread 2 T mixture on bread & broil 2" from heat for 35 seconds. Garnish with scallions.

Salt is the policeman of taste: it keeps the various flavors of then dish in order and restrains the stronger from tyrannizing over the weaker.
          Malcolm de Chazal

appetizers

MARINATED RAW OYSTERS

3 chopped scallions *1 T soy sauce*
¼ t garlic powder *½ t dried basil*
2 T tomato juice *½ t salt*
½ t dried oregano *1 pt oysters*
2 T Italian Dressing

Add all ingredients to drained oysters & mix gently to coat well. Chill covered for 6 hours. Keeps for 4 days.

MUSHROOM, SPINACH & WALNUT PATÉ

¼ C olive oil *2 C spinach*
1 chopped onion *1 ⅓ C walnuts*
1 lb chopped mushrooms *1 C cottage*
1 minced garlic clove   *cheese*
3 T sherry *2 eggs*
¾ t crushed rosemary *⅓ C parsley*
¼ t grated nutmeg

Heat oil & saute the onion, mushrooms & garlic until soft. Add sherry & rosemary & simmer until liquid is absorbed. Put mixture in processor & process with chopped spinach & walnuts until chunky. Add cheese, eggs, chopped parsley & nutmeg. Put into an oiled loaf pan; cover with foil & cook in a pan of water at 375° for 1½ hours. Let cool for ½ hour, then weight down with a plate for 1 hour. Remove from pan & slice; cool. Serve at room temperature. Serve on crackers. Serves 20.

In medieval times, basil was the passport to heaven.

appetizers

TROPICAL SAUSAGE

1½ lb smoked sausage ½ C Coco Lopez
1 T butter 2 T mustard
2 T cornstarch 1 garlic clove
20 oz pineapple chunks 1 bell pepper
8 oz water chestnuts

Cut sausage in ½ inch pieces & brown in butter. Drain. Mix cornstarch, juice from the pineapple, Coco Lopez, mustard & minced garlic & add to sausage. Cook & stir until sauce thickens. Add pineapple, chunks of pepper & water chestnuts & heat through. Makes 40 servings.

FILLED COCKTAIL POPOVERS

Popovers always cause a stir.

1 egg ¼ t salt
½ C flour 1½ t oil
½ C milk Any hot filling

Mix all ingredients except filling in a processor & blend smooth. Grease 16 tiny tart pans & ½ fill with batter. Bake at 400° without peeking for 20 minutes until brown & puffed. Cool on rack & slit each popover on the side & stuff with a filling. Heat filled popovers 5 minutes & serve warm. Makes 16.

HAM FILLING:
1 C ground ham ½ C sour cream
¼ t Dijon mustard 2 T chives

Combine all ingredients. Fill popovers.

CHINESE PORK DIP

2 C pork cubes
1 minced garlic clove
½ t sugar
1 t minced gingerroot

3 T soy sauce
½ t black pepper
1 T oil
Orange Dip

Marinate cubed pork for 2 hours in all remaining ingredients except dip. Bake in a single layer at 325° for 1 hour. Turn several times. Serve with Orange Dip.

ORANGE DIP:
1 C orange marmalade   5 oz horseradish
Combine all. Serves 10.

LASAGNA ROLLUPS

32 oz cottage cheese
½ C parmesan cheese
1 T Italian seasoning
1 beaten egg

12 lasagna
 noodles
8 pieces ham
2 T water

Mix cheeses, Italian seasoning(p.12) & egg. Cook & drain noodles & spread 2 T mixture on each noodle. Top with a ham strip cut in same size as noodle. Starting at narrow end, roll up noodle, being careful to keep filling inside. Place noodles seam side down in greased pan; add water; cover with foil & bake at 400° for 30 minutes. Chill for 3 hours until firm. Slice rolls into 4 pieces & serve. Makes 48.

Some use calendula to make their hair yellow with the flower, not being content with the natural color God has given them.
            William Turner 1551

appetizers 36

TURKEY PATÉ

1 lb ground turkey	1 grated onion
1 C herb season stuffing	2 garlic cloves
½ C chopped parsley	½ t salt
2 minced celery stalks	¼ t pepper
1 grated carrot	1 beaten egg

¼ t poultry seasoning

Mix all the ingredients as well as the minced garlic. Bake in a loaf pan at 350° for 40-45 minutes. Slice & serve warm or cold as a paté. Serves 12.

CURRIED MEATBALLS

1 C soft bread crumbs	1 t salt
28 oz mincemeat	¼ t pepper
1½ lb ground beef	2 t curry powder
1 egg	½ C lemon juice
1 chopped onion	½ C bell pepper

Combine all ingredients & bake at 350° for 1 hour. Serve with toothpicks for an hors d'oevre or with rice for an entree. Serves 6.

PARSLEY PARTY PATÉ

1 env unfl gelatin	½ t Tabasco
10½ oz beef consomme	1 garlic clove
2 cans liver paté	2 t parsley

½ t worcestershire sauce

Dissolve gelatin in warm consomme by placing pan over low heat & stirring. Pour into a small mold & chill 2 hours. Combine remaining ingredients & pack in scooped out center of gelatin, leaving ¼ inch gelatin shell around bottom & sides. Melt gelatin removed from mold; cool & pour over top of paté & chill 'til firm. Unmold & serve on crackers. Serves 10.

appetizers

CURRIED CHICKEN ROLLS

1 ¼ C chopped chicken   3 T mayonnaise
¼ t curry powder   2 T onion
1 C herb croutons   2 T parsley
        8 oz crescent rolls

Mix cooked chicken, curry, 2 T crushed croutons, mayonnaise, chopped onion & parsley. Separate dough in 4 rectangles pressing perforations to seal & roll each to the size 10x5. Spread ¼ of the mix to within ½ inch of edge. Starting at longest side roll up & pinch seams. Cut each roll in 3 pieces. Dip in remaining crushed croutons & place seam down on baking sheet. Bake at 375° 15-20 minutes. Serve warm with a sweet & sour sauce. Makes 12.

HAWAIIAN GINGER CHEESE BALLS

3 oz cream cheese   ½ t soy sauce
1 t grated gingerroot   ½ t sugar
        freshly grated coconut

Mix first 4 ingredients together; chill & form into balls & roll in coconut. Makes 12.

FETA CHEESE SQUARES

For Christina-a delight - she & feta □

2 C biscuit mix   ¼ C parsley
½ C plain yogurt   ½ t dried mint
½ C milk   or oregano
2 eggs   8 oz feta cheese

Mix all together except cheese & beat smooth. Spread in a 9x13 shallow pan & crumble feta cheese evenly on top. Bake at 350° 35-40 minutes. Cool & cut into 1 by 2 inch bars. Makes 50.

appetizers

CHICKEN LICKINS

3 C cooked chicken cubes 1 t salt
½ C melted butter 1 t basil
½ C dry bread crumbs ¼ t thyme
¼ C parmesan cheese 1 t paprika

Dip cooked chicken in butter & then in bread crumbs mixed with all else. Place on sheet & bake at 400° for 15 minutes. Turn halfway through. Serve hot. Makes 24.

STUFFED EDAM CHEESE

1 lb Edam cheese ⅓ C butter
½ t caraway seeds ½ C beer
½ t dry mustard celery salt

Slice top from cheese, Cut around inside edge & carefully scoop out cheese leaving shell intact. Cut cheese in small pieces & blend in processor with other ingredients. Place cheese mixture back in shell. Serve with hunks of dark bread.

CRAB MEAT CRACKERS

8 oz cream cheese 1 T dill
2 minced scallions ¼ t salt
⅛ t cayenne pepper 3 T cream
1½ T horseradish ½ lb crab meat

Beat the cream cheese with the scallions, pepper, horseradish, minced dill, salt & cream. Fold in crab meat. Place in dish & bake at 350° for 25 minutes or until bubbly & light brown on top. Serve hot on crackers or french bread rounds. Serves 6.

appetizers
39

HERBAL CHEESEY CHEESECAKE

2 T butter
1 C zwieback crumbs
11 oz Cheese soup
16 oz cottage cheese
16 oz cream cheese
1½ C grtd cheddar cheese

2 eggs
1 clove garlic
3 T chives
1 C yogurt
½ cucumber
1 t dill

Melt butter & add crumbs. Press firmly on bottom of springform pan. In a processor blend soup, cheeses, eggs, & herbs & beat until smooth. Pour on top of crumbs. Bake at 325° for 1½ hours until puffy. Cool. When ready to serve, spread yogurt over top & garnish with sliced cucumber & snipped dill. Serves 16.

GUACAMOLE CHEESE BALL

6¼ oz Nacho Cheese Sauce
4 oz chopped green chilis
3 C Monterey Jack cheese
1 T minced onion
1 t garlic powder

1 avocado
½ t lemon juice
⅔ C almonds
1 T coriander
Tortilla chips

Mix the cheese sauce, chilis, cheese, onion & garlic powder. Mash avocado with lemon juice & stir into cheese mixture. Chill for 1 hour. Form into a ball & roll in chopped almonds & chopped coriander. Serve with chips.

ROSEMARY PIZZA

Make a bread dough with chopped rosemary in it & roll out as for pizza. Sprinkle with tomato sauce, a dusting of sugar & ½ t dried rosemary. Top with grated mozzarella cheese. Bake at 400° for 20 minutes. Serve hot.

appetizers
40

HERB CHEESE WAFERS

⅓ C bleu cheese
½ C cheddar cheese
¾ C butter

½ clove garlic
1 t parsley
1 t chives
2 C flour

Grate cheeses & cream with butter. Mix in chopped herbs & flour. Shape into 1½" rolls; chill & slice in thin pieces. Bake at 375° for 8-10 minutes. Makes 4 dozen.

DILLY CHEESE TORTE

1½ C bread crumbs
1 C ground almonds
½ C butter
12 oz cream cheese
1 C ricotta cheese
2 eggs

⅓ C dill
2 T cream
1 t lemon rind
1 t salt
½ t grtd nutmeg
dill sprigs

Mix crumbs, almonds & butter & press on bottom & sides of a greased 9" springform pan. In a processor, combine the remaining ingredients except dill sprigs & blend until smooth. Pour into the pan & bake at 350° for 45 minutes until knife in center comes clean. Cool & remove from pan. Garnish with dill sprigs & serve at room temperature. Serves 12.

POTATO CHIP PLATTERS

3 oz Roquefort Cheese
3 oz cream cheese
2 peppercorns

1 clove garlic
6 basil leaves
¼ C parsley

Blend all in processor until smooth. Serve on potato chips or crackers.

FRUIT CHEESE LOG

½ C dried apricots
1 C water
1 lb Monterey Jack
8 oz cream cheese
⅓ C sherry
1 t poppy seeds
½ t garlic salt
⅓ C raisins

Soak apricots in water 2 hours; drain & chop. Blend grated cheeses, sherry & herbs & mix well. Fold in chopped raisins. Shape into a log; wrap & chill until firm. Serve with crackers.

PESTO CAKE

1 env unfl gelatin
¼ C cold water
½ C mayonnaise
8 oz cream cheese
2 T pesto sauce
½ C walnuts

Soften gelatin in water; stir over low heat until dissolved. Add to mayonnaise & mix well. Reserve 2 T gelatin mixture & add rest of gelatin to cream cheese. Combine reserved gelatin with pesto (p. 10). Mix well. Spoon ⅓ cream cheese mixture into oiled 5½ x 3" loaf pan. Cover with half the pesto. Repeat layers, ending with cream cheese. Sprinkle with chopped toasted nuts & press down. Chill until firm. Serve with toasted French bread.

Dioscorides, the Greek herbalist wrote "The herb peony is plucked up in ye heat of ye dog days before the rising of ye sun and it is hanged about one and is good against poisons and heurtings and fears and devils and their assaults, and against a fever that comes with shivering whether by night or by day."

appetizers
42

ZIPPY CRANBERRY CROSTINIS

1½ C cranberries   4 T horseradish
½ C sugar   1 French bread loaf
1 t grated lemon rind   2 T olive oil
          4 oz cream cheese

Cook cranberries in water until skins pop. Drain & mash with sugar, lemon rind & horseradish. Cool. Slice French bread into ½" slices; brush each side with oil & bake at 400° for 8-10 minutes. Cool. To serve, spread toast with cream cheese & top with cranberry mixture. Makes 24.

SERBIAN CHEESE SPREAD

6 oz cream cheese   ¼ C butter
½ C grated feta cheese   1 T cream
1 T minced dill   1 T cut chives
1 T chopped parsley   1 garlic clove

Combine all & beat until blended & fluffy. Cover & chill. Serve on pita bread pieces. Makes 1 cup.

APPLE APPETIZERS

unpeeled red apples   1 T butter
2 oz roquefort cheese   1 T chives
4 oz cream cheese   1 T dry sherry
        ½ C chopped toasted walnuts

Core & section apples. Blend rest of ingredients & spread ½" thick on apples wedges. Sprinkle with walnuts.

a knot garden of salads

The garden sustained the meals of the day
While symbols dominated the borders
Ours had a playhouse, a bay tree, & well
To insure it became family quarters.

salads
44

MOROCCAN ORANGE SALAD

4 peeled oranges
¼ C lemon juice
1 T sugar
¼ t grn. cinnamon
dash salt
½ C radishes
¼ C pitted ripe olives

Cut oranges crosswise into thin sections. Combine lemon juice, sugar & spices & blend well. To serve, overlap oranges, top with sliced radishes & sliced olives & spoon marinade over salad. Serves 8.

GOLDEN RICE SALAD

2 C cooked rice
2 grated carrots
2 oranges, peeled
¼ C lime juice
1 t chives
1 T parsley
1 t salt
½ C salad oil

Cool rice & mix with carrots & sectioned oranges. Combine other ingredients & whisk until blended. Pour over rice mixture and chill. Serves 6.

RIO FESTIVAL SALAD

3 T orange juice
½ t dried oregano
¼ t dried thyme
2 T minced onion
¼ C oil
½ t salt
3 peeled oranges
1 grapefruit
1 # kidney beans
1 C celery
3 T pimento
2 T parsley

Mix juice, oregano, thyme, onion, oil & salt together for dressing. Peel & section oranges & grapefruit; add canned beans, sliced celery, chopped pimento & minced parsley. Pour dressing over salad & chill for several hours. Serve on lettuce. Serves 6.

RED, WHITE AND GREEN SALAD

¼ C oil
2 T cider vinegar
1 garlic clove
¼ t dried dill
1 C watercress leaves

3 C lettuce
1 cucumber
3 bananas
⅛ t salt
⅛ t pepper

1½ C halved cherry tomatoes

Mix oil, vinegar, minced garlic & dill & let sit 1 hour. Cut cress, lettuce, cucumbers & bananas into chunks & add all together. Toss & serve immediately. Serves 8.

PEACHY PEAR SUNDAE SALAD

½ C plain yogurt
2 T sugar
2 t lime juice
½ t grated lime peel
⅛ t ground cardamon

½ C cream
2 pears
2 peaches
2 C lettuce
any sherbet

Mix yogurt, sugar, lime juice & peel & cardamon. Whip cream to soft peaks & fold into yogurt mixture. Cut pears & peeled peaches into chunks & mix with lettuce. Serve in sundae glasses with cardamon dressing poured over evenly & top with a pretty color of sherbet. Serves 6.

The old man attributed his longevity to eating onions and garlic in large quantities. When the angel of death came to call on the thousand year old man, the man said "Whoo-o-o do you want?" and after getting a whiff of his breath the angel went away.

salads

MINTED GRAPEFFRUIT SECTIONS

2 13½ oz frozen grapefruit sections
⅛ t mint extract or 2 t dried mint or 2 T chopped fresh mint
green food coloring

Add mint to grapefruit sections. Add coloring to tint a delicate mint green. Chill. Pineapple chunks may be substituted.

SPICY MOLDED FRUIT

15 ¼ oz pineapple chunks 1 t whole cloves
11 oz mandarin oranges   ¼ t grn. ginger
2 ½ C water   2 env unflavored
1 cinnamon stick   gelatin

Drain fruits & combine juices to make 1 cup. Add to pan with 2 C water, cinnamon stick, cloves & ginger. Simmer 10 minutes & remove spices. In another pan, sprinkle gelatin over remaining water to soften. Add hot spiced liquid; place over low heat & stir until gelatin dissolves. Chill until the consistency of unbeaten egg whites. Fold in any fruits & pour into a 5 cup mold. Chill until firm. Serves 8.

ZUCCHINI-CORN MELANGE

4 julienne zucchini	1 T sugar
3 C cooked corn	2 ½ t basil
1 diced onion	½ t marjoram
2 peppers, chopped	1 t salt
⅓ C cider vinegar	¼ t pepper
1 lemon, juiced	⅔ C oil
1 T Dijon mustard	2 T ketchup
3 cloves garlic	¼ C parsley

Mix the vegetables in a bowl. Mix the dressing ingredients together & whisk in the oil until thickened, Add the ketchup & the minced fresh parsley. Pour over vegetables. Cover & chill overnight. Serves 10-12.

For a quick salad, chop tomatoes & cucumbers; add ½ t oregano, 4 T red vinegar, 1 T oil & 2 T chopped fresh mint leaves. Season with salt & pepper if necessary. Chill before serving.

HERB ASPIC

4 env unfl gelatin	½ C wine vinegar
4 C chicken broth	1 ½ C white wine

2 C chopped parsley, chives, tarragon, chervil, scallions

Sprinkle gelatin over 1 C broth & dissolve over warm heat. Pour into a bowl & stir in remaining broth, vinegar & wine. Chill until syrupy. Fold in any or all of the green herbs. Pour into an oiled 9x13 pan. Chill until firm. Cut in small cubes & serve with ham. Serves 10-12.

salads

A FETA OF TOMATOES

4 chopped tomatoes	2 t basil
1 sliced cucumber	½ t salt
1 C chopped onion	⅔ C feta cheese
3 t oregano	½ C olive oil

Combine tomatoes, cucumber & onion in a bowl & sprinkle with the minced herbs & salt. Cover & chill 30 minutes. Add crumbled cheese & oil & toss. Serves 6.

MIDEASTERN GREEN SALAD

2 C spinach leaves	1 t sugar
2 C lettuce leaves	1½ t mint leaves
2 C watercress	3 T lemon juice
2 C chopped parsley	⅛ t salt
1½ C feta cheese	⅛ t pepper
⅓ C olive oil	1 cucumber

Arrange torn greens & cheese separately on a tray. Mix the rest of the dressing ingredients including the shredded cucumber & blend well. Pour over the leaves as you serve them. Serves 8.

"...What does cooking mean?...It means knowledge of all herbs & fruits & balms & spices & of all that is healing & sweet in groves & savory in meat. It means the knowledge of Medea & of Circe & of Helen & of the Queen of Sheba. It means the economy of your great grandmother, the science of modern chemistry & French art & Arabian hospitality..."

John Ruskin

CHINESE NOODLE SALAD

¼ C vinegar
¼ C soy sauce
4 T sesame oil
2 T minced gingerroot
1 T sugar
½ # thin dried egg noodles

1 cucumber
2 bell peppers
4 stalks celery
½ C coriander
2 C bean sprouts
1 t garlic

Mix vinegar, soy sauce, 3 T sesame oil, grated gingerroot & sugar & let stand 1 hour. Cook noodles al dente & toss with remaining 1 T sesame oil. Peel & slice cucumber ¼" thick. Chop peppers & celery in cubes & add chopped fresh coriander & bean sprouts. Toss all together well. Chill covered for 1 hour. Serves 6.

INDIAN CURRIED SPINACH

¼ C wine vinegar
1½ t curry powder
1 t dry mustard
2 T chutney, chopped
2 t sugar
¼ C oil

½ t salt
2 T green onions
10 oz spinach
½ C peanuts
½ C raisins
1½ C apples

Combine first 7 dressing ingredients in a jar & chill. Slice onions & add with torn fresh spinach in a bowl. Top with peanuts, raisins & chopped unpared apples. Shake dressing & pour over salad. Serves 8.

A good ginger vinaigrette combines:
1 T Dijon mustard
1 T grated gingerroot
4 T chopped scallions
6 turns pepper mill

2 cloves garlic
2 T wine vinegar
2 T cut chives
½ C olive oil

Whisk all together & serve on pasta salad.

salads
50

GINGERED COLE SLAW

1 cabbage head, grated
3 T grated gingerroot
¾ C plain yogurt
¾ C mayonnaise
4½ t Dijon mustard
1 lime, grated
½ C cilantro
⅛ t salt
⅛ t pepper
cherry tomatoes

Grate cabbage. Make dressing with rest of ingredients except tomatoes. Toss all together & chill 4 hours. Serves 12.

POPEYE'S RICE SALAD MOLD

¼ lb fresh spinach
2 cloves garlic
3 t basil
½ t salt
⅛ t pepper
2 T lemon juice
1 T olive oil
3 C cooked rice

Wash & dry fresh spinach & chop in processor with garlic, basil, salt, pepper & juice. Slowly add oil & blend. Combine spinach mixture & rice & mix well. Press into 6 ½ cup molds coated with oil. Cover & chill. Unmold on spinach leaves. Serves 6.

CORNPONE VEGETABLE SALAD

A delicious bread and salad in one pot.

4 C cornbread
1 diced tomato
1 bunch scallions
2 stalks celery
½ C toasted pecans
1 bell pepper
3 oz pimentos
12 basil leaves
½ C yogurt
salt, pepper

Make cornbread from a mix or your favorite recipe in an 8" pan. Crumble when cool. Chop vegetables, nuts & herbs. Mix all with yogurt & coat well. Season to taste. Chill 1 hour. Serves 10-12.

CRACKED WHEAT SALAD

1 C cracked wheat
Warm water
1 bunch green onions
2 bunches parsley
½ C mint leaves

4 tomatoes
8 T lemon juice
¼ C olive oil
¼ C salad oil
Salt & pepper

Soak wheat in water for 1 hour. Squeeze dry by placing plate over wheat & squeezing. Chop onions, herbs & tomatoes finely. Mix all together & serve on lettuce or cabbage. Serves 4.

HERB ASPIC WITH SURPRISES

2 env unfl gelatin
24 oz V-8 juice
½ t chili powder
⅛ t garlic powder
⅛ t ground cumin

⅛ t grn. cloves
1 C green beans
½ C celery
¼ C green pepper
2 T onion

Sprinkle gelatin over ½ C V-8 juice to soften. Warm over low heat until dissolved. Remove from heat & add remaining juice & herbs. Cook beans and add with cut vegetables to aspic. Spoon into 5 cup mold. Chill until firm. Unmold on greens. Serves 4.

MARINATED VEGETABLES WITH FENNEL

1 lb mushrooms, 10 tomatoes, 1 green pepper
Marinade:
2 T olive oil, 2 chopped shallots, 1 minced clove garlic, 1 t crushed coriander & fennel seeds, 2 T white wine, ½ lemon, juiced, 1¼ C water.

Heat the oil. add the remaining ingredients & cook until reduced. Pour over vegetables & marinate for 1 hour.

salads

OREGON BLEU CHEESE POTATO SALAD

¼ C cider vinegar	12 potatoes
2 t Dijon mustard	½ C watercress
8 turns pepper mill	½ C bleu cheese
⅔ C olive oil	½ C cream
¼ C minced shallots	12 slices bacon
2 T minced parsley	3 T cut chives

Mix vinegar, mustard & pepper. Whisk in oil until thick. Add shallots & parsley. Cook potatoes until tender. Cut in ¼ " slices & mix with ½ C dressing. Line platter with lettuce. Alternate rows of potatoes & chopped watercress. Whisk cheese & cream into remaining dressing. Spoon over potatoes. Top with cooked, crumbled bacon & chopped chives. Serve warm or at room temperature. Serves 15.

GREEN BEAN POTATO VINAIGRETTE

2 C new potatoes	1 T dill
2 C green beans	½ t pepper
⅓ C olive oil	¼ C green olives
1 T Dijon mustard	¼ C black olives
1 T lemon juice	1 T capers
1 T wine vinegar	1 head lettuce

Cook small potatoes 3 minutes; add green beans & cook 4 minutes longer. Whisk liquids & herbs together & add cut up vegetables, sliced olives & capers. Toss. Serve on lettuce cups. Serves 4.

Better is a dinner of herbs where love is than a fatted ox and hatred with it.

           Proverbs 15:17

CANTALOPE WITH CURRIED SHRIMP SALAD

1 C plain yogurt
¼ C minced parsley
¼ t salt
¼ t curry powder

1 T lemon juice
2 cantalopes
1 lb shrimp
½ C grapes

Mix yogurt, parsley, salt, curry & juice. Chill. Cut cantalopes in half & fill with cooked & chilled shrimp & grapes. Serve with chilled dressing. Serves 4.

SHRIMP AND AVOCADO SALAD

½ C red bell pepper
3 T olive oil
3 T wine vinegar
½ C chopped onion
1 T candied ginger

1 ¼ lb shrimp
1 t salt
¼ t black pepper
1 avocado, sliced
2 T chopped dill

Cut the pepper in strips & blanch for 2 minutes in boiling water. Heat the oil & vinegar & add the onion, chopped candied ginger, the cleaned shrimp, salt & pepper. Cook the mixture just until shrimp turns pink. Add the avocado & red pepper. Sprinkle with dill & serve immediately. Serves 6.

SMOKED FISH SALAD

8 oz cream cheese
⅓ C chopped onion
1 T Dijon mustard
1 T sour cream
salt & pepper

2 t dill weed
1 t horseradish
1 T parsley
1 T mayonnaise
7 oz smoked fish

In large bowl mix all ingredients except fish. Gently fold in any fish (tuna, mackerel). Arrange on greens & garnish with onion rings or tomatoes. Serves 4.

salads
54

CRAB AND BASIL SALAD

10½ oz tomato soup
1 pkg unflavored gelatin
¼ C cold water
1 C cottage cheese
½ C mayonnaise
¼ C cream, whipped

½ C green pepper
½ C celery
2 T chives
3 t basil
1 cucumber
2 C crab meat

Heat soup; add gelatin which has been softened in cold water. Add cottage cheese & cool. Add mayonnaise, whipped cream, chopped vegetables & herbs & crab. Pour into ring mold. Chill until firm.

DRESSING

8 oz cream cheese
2 T lemon juice

1 C cream
1 C green olives

Whip all together & serve in center of ring mold. Serves 8-10.

SPICED BOSTON BEET RING

8 oz cream cheese
2 T toasted sesame seed

1 qt borscht
1 T pickle spice

6 oz lemon Jello

Shape cream cheese into 12 1" balls & roll in sesame seeds. Strain borscht & save beets. Measure 2 cups of beet juice; add pickling spice & simmer 10 minutes. Remove spice. Measure liquid from pan & add hot water to make 2 cups. Pour over Jello, stirring to dissolve. Add cold water to beet juice to make 2 cups & stir into Jello. Stir reserved beets into mixture & pour into mold. Place cream cheese balls carefully in pattern in mold. Chill until firm. Serve with sour cream. Serves 8.

AVOCADO, APRICOT, CHICKEN SALAD

3 C cubed cooked chicken
1 ½ C slivered apricots
⅓ C sliced celery
¼ C sliced scallions
⅓ C mayonnaise
⅓ C yogurt
1 T vermouth
½ t lemon rind
⅛ t grt nutmeg
1 sliced avocado
1 T lime juice
Lettuce
¼ C toasted sliced almonds

Mix chicken chunks, apricots, celery & scallions. Mix the next 5 ingredients for a dressing & combine with chicken, tossing until well coated. Cover & chill for 3 hours to blend flavors. Brush avocado with lime juice. Divide salad between 4 plates & garnish with avocado & sprinkle with almonds. Serves 4.

CHICKEN & HERBS IN A PEA POD

¼ C mayonnaise
¼ C yogurt
2 t grated gingerroot
2 C breaded chicken
½ C celery
¼ lb pea pods
½ t lime peel
Salt & pepper
¼ lb soft herb cheese food

Mix mayonnaise, yogurt, ginger & stir in cooked, cubed chicken, sliced celery, blanched Chinese pea pods, grated lime peel & seasoning to taste. Cube cheese, fold in just before serving. Serves 4.

Borage flowers were put into wine to "make men & women glad & merry & drive away all sadness, dullness & melancholy & quieteth the lunatic & cardiac passion of hearts."

Gerard

salads

SINGPORE COLD POULTRY

3 C raw chicken
2½ C chicken stock
1 lb very thin spaghetti
5 T peanut oil
1 large honeydew melon
2 mangoes
1 bunch scallions

1 diced onion
2 cloves garlic
10 oz gingerroot
¾ C crunchy peanut butter
¼ C Coco Lopez
1¼ C water

juice of 1 lime

Cook chicken in stock & cut in big chunks. Reserve 1¼ cups stock. Cook spaghetti just until al dente. Drain & toss with 4 T peanut oil. Peel & cut the melon & mangoes the same size as the chicken. Cut the scallions into shreds & add to the pasta. To make the sauce, heat the remaining 1 T oil & fry the onion, minced garlic, & grated ginger until soft. Add crunchy peanut butter, reserved chicken stock, Coco Lopez & water & stir over heat. Whisk until smooth & add lime juice. Cool but do not chill. Divide the pasta, top with chicken, mango & melon & serve with the sauce separately. Serves 14 as a salad & 8 as a main course.

KIELBASA SALAD

1 lb kielbasa
2 C cooked lentils
1 chopped green pepper
3 hard boiled eggs

1 chopped onion
3 tomatoes
1 t basil
Italian Dressing

Broil kielbasa for 5 minutes. Cut in thin slices & add to all other ingredients in a bowl & coat with Italian Dressing. Toss & serve on lettuce, garnished with egg slices. Serves 6.

ST PATRICK'S DILLY SALAD

My teenager loves this different salad.

8 oz cooked egg noodles	¼ C oil
7 oz corned beef	¼ C vinegar
3 hard boiled eggs	½ T sugar
1 T worcestershire sauce	1 t dill weed
3 tomatoes, cut	½ t garlic salt
¼ C sliced olives	

Drain noodles well; cube corned beef, slice eggs & mix all together. Cover and chill for 2 hours, tossing occasionally. Serves 8.

HERBAL GREEN SALAD

1 minced garlic clove	1 T vinegar
2 t chopped chives	1 t salt
¼ t ea tarragon, chervil	¾ t dill
½ t ea mustard, paprika	⅓ C oil
½ C buttermilk	1 C yogurt

Process garlic, chives, herbs, buttermilk & vinegar & process while adding oil slowly. Blend in yogurt. Store tightly covered in refrigerator. Will keep for a week. Pour over vegetables or greens. Makes 2 cups.

Pliny tells us "Mint was once the nymph Menthe who attracted the roving eye of Pluto. Pluto's wife, in a jealous frenzy, knocked her down & was in the process of trampling her to death when Pluto appeared and turned Menthe into a delightful herb - even sacred to him."

salads
58

MAPLE CHICKEN SALAD

½ C maple syrup   1 t sage
¼ C chopped walnuts   ¼ C raisins
¼ C cider vinegar   ½ t ginger
3 C cooked cubed chicken 1 diced apple

Mix together & serve with any dressing.

SALAD SEASONING

¾ C Parmesan cheese   1 t chives
¼ C parsley flakes   1 t basil
1 t bell pepper flakes   ½ t salt
1 t garlic powder   ½ t pepper

Mix ingredients & store in a air tight container. Sprinkle on tossed green salad, sliced zucchini or cucumber tomato salad. Makes 1 cup.

SESAME CARAMEL CHIPS

Melt ¼ C sugar & 1 T sesame seeds in heavy pan over low heat until golden. Pour on oiled sheet & break into chips when cool. Serve on fruit salads.

A good ginger vinaigrette combines:
1 T Dijon mustard   2 cloves garlic
1 T grated gingerroot   2 T wine vinegar
4 T chopped scallions   2 T cut chives
6 turns pepper mill   ½ C olive oil

Whisk all together & serve on pasta salad.

a simple of soups

THE HERBALIST.

locally in diseases of the skin. The flowers are used in Germany for dyeing yellow.

YERBA SANTA
(Eriodictyon Californicum).

Common Names—Mountain Balm, Consumptives' Weed, Tarweed, Bearsweed, Holy Herb.

Medicinal Part—The leaves.

Description—This evergreen shrub is a member of the Waterleaf family, 3 to 4 feet high. Stem smooth but exudes a gummy substance. The leaves are glutinous, 3 to 4 inches in length, alternately on stem, oblong, or oval, lance-shaped, narrowing gradually to a short stalk; margins toothed except at base; upper surface smooth with depressed veins; the under side contains a network of prominent veins and is covered with a resinous substance making them appear as if varnished. Flowers whitish or pale blue in clusters at top of plant. The seed capsule is oval, greyish brown and contains small reddish brown shriveled seeds.

Properties and Uses—Yerba Santa is an excellent expectorant and valuable in asthma and throat and bronchial troubles. It is also used as a tonic. It has an aromatic odor and sweetish balsamic taste.

Dose—Steep a teaspoonful of the leaves into a cup of boiling water for half an hour. Drink a half cupful at night upon retiring hot or cold—or take a mouthful 3 times a day. 1 or 2 cupfuls may be taken. Tincture 10 to 30 min.

A simple is a subtle or a complex cure,
From asafoetida to sage on mutton;
And if you desire to conceive a child,
Put tansy in your belly button.

soups

GOLDEN GAZPACHO

3 red bell peppers
½ C concentrated
  orange juice
4 T grtd orange rind
½ t cayenne pepper
¾ C bread crumbs

2 garlic cloves
¼ C lemon juice
2 cucumbers
1 onion
⅓ C olive oil
½ t salt

Combine all ingredients in a processor. Puree until smooth. Chill. Serves 6.

CHILLED LEMON SOUP

10¾ oz cream of
  chicken soup
1 C chicken stock

1 C milk
3 T mint leaves
2 T lemon juice

Parsley for garnish

Combine all ingredients except parsley garnish in a processor. Puree until smooth. Soup must be served icy cold. Garnish with chopped parsley. Serves 4.

LAVENDER BLUE SOUP

Pretty enough for a lady going to Scarborough Faire.

4 pints blueberries
2 C maple syrup
1 T lemon juice

6 lavender stems
2 C buttermilk
2 C cream

Simmer the blueberries, syrup & lemon juice for 30 minutes. Put in a processor. Puree until smooth. Chill. Soak the lavender in the buttermilk & cream for 1 hour. Remove the sprigs. Combine the 2 liquids & chill for 4 hours. Serve cold to 8 people with lavender blossoms.

THANKSGIVING CRANBERRY SOUP

12 oz cranberries
3 C water
1¼ C sugar
2 cinnamon sticks
2 allspice berries
2 whole cloves
4 peppercorns
1 T cornstarch
¼ C cream
¾ C red wine

Bring cranberries, water, sugar & spices to a boil & simmer 20 minutes. Mix cornstarch with 2 T water & whisk this into soup. Heat until thickened. Chill. When serving, stir in the cream & wine. Serves 6.

PRETTY AS A PEACH SOUP

4 peaches
½ t almond extract
1 C plain yogurt
1 T lemon juice
4 mint sprigs for garnish

Peel peaches; dice 2 & cut 2 in chunks. Combine chunks, extract, yogurt & lemon juice in a processor. Puree until smooth. Stir diced peaches into soup. Chill. Garnish with mint sprigs.

SPICED MELON MELANGE SOUP

1 cantalope, cubed
3 C orange juice
2 T lime juice
½ t cinnamon

Combine all ingredients in a processor. Puree until smooth. Chill. Serves 4.

soups
62

GREAT GRAPE GAZPACHO

2 C seedless grapes	¼ C olive oil
3 slices bread	1 T vinegar
2 C cold water	salt & pepper
¼ t almond extract	2 garlic gloves
½ C blanched almonds	2 T chives

Remove stems from grapes. Cube bread & cover with water; soak until soft. Combine all ingredients except chives in processor & puree until smooth. Chill 1 hour. Serve with chopped chives. Serves 4.

A WISE SAGE & GARLIC SOUP

7 cloves garlic, halved	1 bay leaf
4 C water	1 egg yolk
salt & pepper	3 T olive oil
sprigs of sage & thyme	French bread

Add garlic to water with salt & pepper to taste & herbs. Cook for 20 minutes; remove the herbs. Beat the egg yolk & pour the soup slowly over the egg beating constantly. Drizzle oil over slices of bread & place in a soup bowl. Serve soup hot on bread. Serves 4.

JELLIED CUCUMBER & MINT SOUP

1 shallot	2 T lemon juice
1 cucumber	1 pkg unflavored gelatin
3¾ chicken stock	3 T mint

Chop the shallot & grate the peeled cucumber & cook in heated chicken stock. Add salt & pepper if necessary. Stir in lemon juice. Dissolve gelatin in a little of the stock & return to soup. Chill. When half set, add chopped mint & chill again. Spoon into cups when ready to serve.

DILLY CARROT SOUP

2 T olive oil
1 C chopped onions
5 C diced carrots
4 C chicken stock
½ t salt
⅛ t pepper
¼ C cottage cheese
2 T port wine
2 T dill

Heat the oil & saute the onion until wilted. Add carrots, stock, salt & pepper & cook on low for 30 minutes. Combine the solids in a processor with the cheese & 1 C of the broth. Puree until smooth. Return the puree & the remaining liquid back to the pan & bring to a boil. Add the port & chopped dill. Serve hot or cold. Serves 6.

VEGETABLE PESTO SOUP

3 qts water
2 C sliced carrots
2 C sliced celery
2 C diced potatoes
2 C diced onions
2 C sliced green beans
2 C shredded cabbage
2 C navy beans
2 sliced zucchini
1 diced pepper
½ C macaroni
Salt & pepper
4 T garlic
¼ C tomato paste
¼ C basil
¼ C parsley
½ C olive oil
½ C parmesan cheese

Bring water to a boil & cook carrots, celery, potatoes, & onions for 30 minutes. Add beans, cabbage, zucchini, bell pepper, & macaroni & cook 20 more minutes. Add salt & pepper to taste. Prepare the pesto by mashing the garlic & adding all else to make a paste. To serve, ladle into a bowl & slowly stir in the pesto. Serve with extra parmesan cheese & bread. Serves 12.

Woe to the cook whose sauce has no sting. Chaucer

SWEDISH SPLIT PEA SOUP

Swedes eat this soup on Thursday as King Eric in 1577 died on Thursday after his brother poisoned his soup. Good luck!

1½ C split peas	2 onions
10 C water	1 t marjoram
1 lb piece of ham	pinch ginger

Wash & soak beans overnight. Discard water. Cook in 10 C water for 2 hours, removing skins as they float to surface. Add all else; season to taste. Serves 6.

GARDEN DILL CHOWDER

Use frozen vegetables if your garden has stopped producing.

1 chopped onion	2 C milk
1 chopped green pepper	10 oz broccoli
2 T olive oil	& cauliflower
21 oz cream potato soup	10 oz corn
2 C chicken broth	1 T dill
8 slices cooked chopped bacon	

Saute onion & pepper in oil until soft. Stir in soup, broth & milk & bring to a boil. Add frozen vegetables & simmer covered 12 minutes until tender. Add chopped dill & bacon & serve hot. Serves 8-10.

An herbal advent wreath has rosemary for remembrance, sage for immortality, lavender for purity & virtue of Mary and thyme and lady's bedstraw for association with the manger.

SHAKER HERB SOUP

1 T olive oil	2 T chives
2 T chervil	2 T sorrel
½ t tarragon	1 C celery
1 qt chicken broth	6 slices toast
salt & pepper	grated cheddar cheese
½ t sugar	grated nutmeg

Heat oil & add chervil & tarragon. Saute 3 minutes. Add broth, celery & seasonings. Simmer 30 minutes. Place toast in bowls & pour soup over. Garnish with cheese & nutmeg. Serve very hot. Serves 6.

GERMAN BEER BROTH AND DUMPLINGS

¼ C butter	¼ t grnd ginger
3 sliced onions	2½ C beer
¼ t salt	5 C beef stock
¼ t grnd cinnamon	4 eggs
	2 t grated lemon rind

Dumplings:

2 C flour	4 oz suet
pinch of salt & pepper	1 T parsley
	⅔ C water

Melt butter & cook onions until transparent. Stir in seasonings, beer & stock & bring to a boil. Make dumplings by mixing ingredients to form a soft dough. Shape in small balls with floured hands & drop dumplings in broth. Cover & simmer 10 minutes. Uncover & simmer 10 minutes. Lift out dumplings & keep warm. Mix a little broth with eggs then pour into remaining broth. Stir well. Add lemon rind & serve with dumplings on top. Serves 10.

All herbs except bay leaves loose flavor if cooked too long.

LEMON CURRIED SOUP

2 T oil
2 chopped shallots
1½ t chopped lemon balm
1 t curry powder
6 turns pepper mill

1 T flour
1½ pts chicken stock
2 T lemon juice
½ C cream
1 T chopped coriander

Heat the oil & fry shallots until soft. Add lemon balm, curry, pepper & flour stirring constantly. Pour in stock & bring to a boil. Lower the heat & stir in lemon juice & cream. Add salt if needed. Put ingredients in a processor. Puree until smooth. Chill & garnish with coriander.

HERBED CUCUMBER SOUP

1 peeled cucumber
1½ C yogurt
1½ C buttermilk
¼ C chopped parsley

1 garlic clove
2 T chives
2 T dill
½ C walnuts

salt & pepper to taste

Combine all in a processor. Puree until smooth. Chill. Garnish with chopped walnuts. Serves 6.

PUMPKIN BASIL SOUP

1 lb cubed pumpkin
½ lb sliced carrots
3¾ C chicken stock
1 chopped onion
¼ C butter

½ lb tomatoes
¼ t salt
pinch of sugar
⅛ t pepper
2 T basil

Put pumpkin & carrots in stock & simmer covered for 20 minutes. Stir onions in butter until soft. Add chopped tomatoes & cook until mushy. Combine all ingredients in a processor. Puree. Serve hot to 6.

GUACAMOLE SOUP

2 diced avocados
1 medium diced onion
1 t minced garlic
4 oz green chilis
1 T lime juice
2 C chicken stock

½ C yogurt
½ C milk
¼ t cayenne pepper
½ t salt
3 T cilantro
Strips of fried tortilla

Combine all but strips in a processor. Puree smooth. Chill. Garnish with tomatoes & tortillas. Serves 6.

CORIANDER CARROT SOUP

¼ C butter
2 lb sliced carrots
2 sliced potatoes
1 sliced onion
6 C chicken stock
2 t coriander seeds

½ t grn ginger
½ t grn mace
¼ t salt
⅛ t pepper
⅔ C milk
⅔ C cream

Melt butter & saute vegetables until soft but not brown. Add stock & crushed seeds & seasonings. Simmer 40 minutes until vegetables are cooked. Put all ingredients in a processor. Puree until smooth. Reheat & serve immediately. Serves 10.

DILL SEED WITH PUMPKIN SOUP

2 lb cubed pumpkin
2 T sugar
2 C chicken stock
2 t dill seeds

pepper to taste
salt to taste
1 C yogurt
½ t cinnamon

Boil pumpkin & sugar in water to cover. Drain. Combine with stock in a processor. Puree smooth. Add the dill seeds. Heat & serve with a spoonful of yogurt & a dusting of cinnamon. Serves 6.

soups
68

CHICKEN PEANUT STEW

3 C cubed chicken   8 C water
1 T salt   1 tomato
8 oz tomato sauce   ¼ t cayenne
1 sliced onion   1 T thyme
           ½ lb peanut butter

Cook first 4 ingredients until soft. Add water, whole tomato & seasonings. After 5 minutes take ½ C stock & add to peanut butter. Mix well & add to soup. Simmer 1 hour or until chicken is done. Serves 6.

SALMON DILL SOUP

1 C chopped onions   1 C carrots
2 T butter   1 t dill weed
1 C cubed potatoes   1 T vinegar
21 oz chicken broth   1 t sugar
16 oz stewed tomatoes   16 oz salmon
½ t salt   1 C sour cream

Saute onions in butter. Add all other ingredients except salmon & sour cream & boil 30 minutes. Add fish; simmer 4 minutes & serve with a spoonful of sour cream on top. Serves 8-10.

WINTER PARSLEY PUREE

1 T butter   ½ C grated potato
¾ C minced parsley   1 t chervil
1 C chicken broth   ¾ C milk
           pinch of nutmeg

Melt butter; add parsley & cook until wilted. Add broth, potato & chervil; cover & simmer 20 minutes. Puree in processor; add all else. Reheat. Serves 3.

POTATO AND CHEESE SWIRL SOUP

3 sliced onions
2 T butter
4 C sliced potatoes
½ C sliced celery
3 C chicken broth
1 C watercress
¼ C parsley
¼ C dill
½ C water
8 oz roquefort cheese
1 C cream

Saute onions in butter until soft. Add vegetables & broth & simmer 20 minutes. Puree mixture in processor. Measure 1 C of this puree & combine with herbs & water & simmer covered 15 minutes. Add cheese & process again. Add ¾ C cream to potato mixture & remaining ¼ C cream to roquefort mix. Season with salt & pepper. Chill. When serving, pour potato mixture into tureen & pour roquefort in center. Swirl to form attractive design. Garnish with watercress. Serves 10.

BEAN CACHEPOT

1 lb cooked navy beans
1 T oil
⅔ C chopped onion
1 minced garlic clove
½ lb cubed pork
1 ¼ lb cubed chicken
1 C chicken broth
½ C white wine
½ t thyme
3 whole cloves
1 bay leaf
½ lb sausage
¼ t salt
⅛ t pepper
⅓ C bread crumbs
½ C parsley

Cook beans. Heat oil & saute onion & garlic until soft. Brown pork & chicken in same pan. Mix broth, wine & herbs. In baking dish, layer beans, onion mixture & cooked sausage. Pour wine mixture over casserole; season with salt & pepper. Bake at 350° for 1 hour. Stir & top with crumbs & minced parsley. Serves 6.

soups
70

CURRIED APPLE SOUP

10¾ oz cream of chicken soup
15 oz applesauce
13¾ oz chicken broth
curry powder to taste

Combine all ingredients in a pan & heat through. Serve hot or cold. Serves 4-6.

RED KIDNEY BEAN SOUP

1 T butter	1 t grnd cumin
1½ C chopped onions	8 turns pepper mill
1 C chopped celery	¼ t salt
1 T chopped garlic	1 bay leaf
1 lb kidney beans	1 t thyme
2 smoked ham hocks	8 C water
2 C chicken stock	1 T lemon juice
1 t chili powder	2 T wine vinegar

Melt butter & saute onions, celery & garlic until soft. Combine all ingredients excpt lemon juice & vinegar & simmer covered 1½ hours. Remove bay leaf & ham hocks & cut away meat. In a processor, puree until smooth. Add lemon juice & vinegar & reheat. Serves 10.

COLD CURRY SOUP

6 peeled tomatoes	1 T parsley
½ onion	¼ t sugar
½ t salt	1 t curry
4 turns of pepper mill	4 T mayonnaise

Combine all ingredients in a processor. Puree until smooth. Chill. Serves 4.

a wreath of breads

Christmas at "Boxley,"   *Newport News, Virginia*

'Twas pennyroyal blossomed that night
The angels came to earth
And o'er the stall at Bethlehem
Proclaimed our Saviour's birth.

And thyme was on sweet Mary's bed
To bring her courage rare;
While shepherds lifted up their hearts
In silent joyful prayer.

And now in fond remembrance of
That night so long ago,
I add this sprig of rosemary
To keep his love aglow.
              Anonymous

AUTUMN BUNDT BREAD

10 T butter	½ t nutmeg
1½ C sugar	¼ t grnd cloves
2 C flour	¼ t grnd ginger
1 T baking powder	2 eggs
½ t baking soda	1 C pumpkin
½ t salt	2 C apples
½ t cinnamon	1 C pecans

Cream butter & sugar. Add dry ingredients, beating just until moistened. Add eggs, pumpkin, shredded unpeeled apples & chopped pecans. Mix just until blended. Pour into a greased bundt pan & bake at 350° for 60 minutes. Cool.

LEMON HERB LOAF

This wonderful bread uses that invasive lemon balm in your herb garden.

6 T butter	1 T lemon balm
1 C sugar	¾ C milk
2 eggs	2 C flour
1 T grtd lemon rind	2t baking powder
1 T lemon thyme	¼ t salt

Cream butter & sugar. Add eggs & grated rind. Add chopped herbs to milk & heat until hot. Steep 30 minutes. Add dry ingredients alternately with milk, beating just until moistened. Pour into a greased 9x5x3 pan & bake at 325° for 50 minutes. Cool. A sugar, lemon juice mixture can be poured over if desired.

Mint Sandwich Spread - Mix ½ C salad dressing with 1 C chopped walnuts & ½ C chopped mint leaves. Delicious & cooling.

INDIAN TEA BREAD

2 C raisins	1 T butter
1 C currants	2 C flour
2 T candied ginger	1 T grnd ginger
1½ C strong tea	1 t baking soda
1 egg	¼ t nutmeg
¼ C molasses	½ C walnuts

½ C sunflower seeds

Combine raisins, currants, chopped candied ginger & tea & let stand 30 minutes. Add the egg, molasses, & melted butter & blend. Mix dry ingredients & add all together beating just until moistened. Pour into a greased 9x5x3 pan & bake at 350° for 50 minutes. Cool 10 minutes & remove from pan. This bread slices better the second day.

LUNCHBOX VITAMIN BREAD

½ C crunchy peanut butter	¼ t cinnamon
½ C honey	¼ t grnd cloves
3 T oil	¼ t grnd nutmeg
½ C grated carrots	1 t vanilla
1 mashed banana	pinch salt
¼ C milk	1 t soda
1 t baking powder	2 eggs

1 ¾ C whole wheat flour

Mix peanut butter, honey, oil, fruits & milk. Add dry ingredients & vanilla, beating just until moistened. Add eggs.
Pour into a greased loaf pan & bake at 350° for 60 minutes. Cool.

Make an onion & parsley finger sandwich by mixing lots of both together with salt to enhance flavor. Spread on bread.

breads
74

SHAKER HERB BREAD

1 C milk	1 egg
2 T sugar	1 T herbs (sage,
¼ t salt	rosemary, cara-
2 T butter	way seed, nutmeg)
1 env dry yeast	4 C flour

Scald the milk & add to sugar, salt & butter. Cool to lukewarm. Add yeast & stir until dissolved. Add egg & a mixture of herbs & 2 cups flour. Beat until smooth. Add remaining flour to make a stiff dough that won't stick to the bowl. Knead until smooth & elastic. Form into a ball, put in greased bowl, covered & let rise until doubled. Punch down & put into a greased loaf pan. Let rise again until bread fills the pan & bake at 425° for 15 minutes. Reduce heat to 375° & bake another 35 minutes. Cool.

IRISH HERB BREAD

This will bring the leprechauns to your door.

1 C unbleached flour	¼ t oregano
1 C whole wheat flour	½ t basil
½ C sugar	pinch thyme
½ t salt	¼ C nuts
1½ t soda	1 egg
¾ C raisins	½ C buttermilk
½ t mayonnaise	1 T butter

Mix all ingredients until moistened. Add more buttermilk if needed to make a stiff dough. Knead lightly & place dough ball on a well greased cookie sheet. Cut an X in the top to "keep the devil out." Bake at 375° for 30-40 minutes.

PUMPKIN BRAN CORNBREAD

1 C cooked pumpkin	½ C cornmeal
½ C milk	½ C flour
2 eggs	4 T bran cereal
4 T butter	2 t baking powder
4 T honey	½ t baking soda

2 t pumpkin pie spice

Mix the first 5 moist ingredients together. Stir the next 6 dry ingredients together & add to the pumpkin mix. Pour into a greased loaf pan & bake at 350° for 50 minutes.

BREAKFAST CORNBREAD

4 T melted butter	1 C flour
1 C buttermilk	1½ t soda
1 egg	¼ t salt
1½ t baking powder	1 t thyme
1 C yellow cornmeal	⅓ C fried bacon

Mix butter, buttermilk & egg. Add dry ingredients, beating just until moistened. Crumble bacon on top of mixture. Pour into a greased 8" square pan & bake at 425° for 20 minutes or until firm to the touch. Cool. Cut into fingers or squares.

HERB BREAD STICKS

2 t caraway seeds	½ t nutmeg
1 pkg hot roll mix	1 t sage

Mix all ingredients together. Prepare as directions on mix. Let rise until doubled. Shape into 24 bread sticks. Place on greased cookie sheets 1" apart. Let rise until light - 30-60 minutes. Bake at 400° for 15 minutes. Makes 24.

breads

SUNSET TOMATO LOAF

¼ C warm water	2 T oil
1 pkg dry yeast	1 t salt
1 C tomato juice	3 C flour
1 T chopped parsley	1 egg,
1 T chopped oregano	separated
2 T sugar	1 t water

Put water in bowl & add yeast to soften. Add all else but the egg white & 1 t water. Beat well. Add more flour if necessary while kneading to make smooth. Place in greased bowl & let rise covered for 50 minutes. Punch down, divide in half & roll each half into a long loaf. Place in greased baguette pan. Cover & let rise until doubled. Brush tops with mixture of egg white & 1 t water. Slash loaves in center with a knife. Bake at 375° for 35-40 minutes. Cool.

LEMON TEA MUFFINS

1 C butter	½ t salt
1 C sugar	½ C lemon juice
4 eggs, separated	¼ C pecans
2 C flour	2 T brown sugar
2 t baking powder	¼ t nutmeg

Cream butter & sugar. Add egg yolks & dry ingredients, beating just until moistened. Add lemon juice. Beat egg whites until stiff but not dry. Fold into mixture. Pour into a greased muffin tins ¾ full. Combine chopped nuts, brown sugar & nutmeg & sprinkle over muffins. Bake at 375° for 15-20 minutes. Cool. Makes 18.

Variation: Add 1¼ C blueberries to batter.

AN APPLE A DAY MUFFIN

¼ C oil
½ C sugar
1 egg
¼ C crunchy peanut butter
1½ C flour
3 t baking powder
½ t salt
½ t cinnamon
⅔ C milk
1 C apple
¼ C raisins
Topping

TOPPING: ¼ C crunchy peanut butter, ⅓ C chopped nuts, ⅓ C brown sugar.

Cream oil & sugar. Add egg & peanut butter. Add dry ingredients, alternately with milk, beating just until moistened. Fold in chopped apples & raisins. Sprinkle with mixed topping. Pour into greased muffin pans ⅔ full & bake at 375° for 25 minutes. Makes 12.

WINTERTIME SUNSHINE MUFFINS

½ C raisins
½ C warm water
1 egg
⅓ C sugar
¼ C oil
⅛ t vanilla extract
⅛ t lemon extract
1 C applesauce
1¾ C flour
1 t soda
1 t grn cinnamon
½ t grn nutmeg
½ t salt
¾ C coconut
¾ C grtd carrots

Mix raisins with water & soak. Cream egg, sugar & oil. Add extracts & applesauce. Add dry ingredients, beating just until moistened. Fold in grated coconut, carrots, & raisins with their water. Spoon into a greased muffin cups & bake at 400° for 15 minutes or until brown. Makes 12.

GERMANTOWN PUFFS

These delicate little mouthfuls resemble popovers with their custard like middle.

3 eggs, separated	½ t salt
5 T flour	1 C milk
1½ t melted butter	¼ t nutmeg
½ t ground cinnamon	

Beat the eggs separately & combine. Add the remaining ingredients. Pour into greased patty pans & bake at 450° until puffs have risen- 5 minutes & then 350° until done.

PAUL BUNYON TOAST

¾ C flour	½ t salt
1 t baking powder	2 T sugar
1 T cinnamon	2 eggs
1 t grtd nutmeg	1 C milk
1 t grnd cloves	2 T oil
1 t grnd ginger	8 slices bread

Mix the dry ingredients together. Mix the eggs, milk & oil & add to rest, mixing just until combined. Batter should be as thick as heavy cream. Thin with milk if necessary. Dip bread slices in batter & fry on griddle as for pancakes. Serve with syrup. Serves 4.

LEMON MINT BUTTER

1 C butter	2 T mint leaves
1 T grated lemon peel	

Mix ingredients in a processor and store in refrigerator. This is especially good on nut bread.

ASTRONAUT'S SWEET ROLLS

1 T orange drink mix
2 T orange marmalade
¼ C pecans
2 T coconut
8 oz can crecent rolls

Mix first 4 ingredients & spread on long dough. Roll up like a jellyroll. Cut in 12 slices. Bake at 350° for 12 minutes.

SPICY BREAKFAST PUFFS

18 ¼ oz yellow cake mix
1 t nutmeg
¾ C water
¼ C oil
1 egg
3 T butter
⅓ C sugar
1 T cinnamon

Combine cake mix, nutmeg, water, oil & egg & mix well. Spoon into greased muffin pans filling ⅔ full. Bake at 350° for 25-30 minutes until toothpick comes clean. Melt butter. Mix sugar & cinnamon. Dip muffin tops in butter then into sugar mix. Makes 18 puffs.

CANDIED GINGER BISCUITS

½ C butter
⅓ C brown sugar
2 T molasses
¼ C apple cider
2 C flour
1 T grnd ginger
½ t soda
½ C candied ginger

Cream butter & sugar. Add molasses & cider. Add dry ingredients & chopped candied ginger, beating just until moistened. Wrap & chill 1 hour. Roll out dough on a floured board. Cut into biscuits & place on a greased cookie sheet. Bake at 350° for 15 minutes. Makes 16-20 biscuits.

breads

HERBAL TOAST

½ C butter
¼ t thyme
¼ t oregano
¼ t black pepper

¼ t garlic
½ t salt
½ t shallots
1 t parsley

Chop all & mix together. Dip bread fingers in herb butter. Bake at 350° 20 minutes.

DILLY CHEESE LOAF

1 loaf French bread
½ C butter
⅓ C onions
3 T mustard

1 T dill seeds
2 t lemon juice
dash Tabasco
12 Swiss Cheese

6 slices crumbled bacon

Cut off top & side crusts of bread & slice into 10 slices. Mix next 6 ingredients & let stand. Cut each slice of Swiss Cheese into 2 triangles & place one long side down in each cut of bread. Place next triangle so that point falls over top of cut in the bread. Make sure each cut has 2 triangles of cheese. Spread butter mixture over loaf & sprinkle with crisp, crumbled bacon. Heat for 30 minutes at 350°.

RYE HERB LOAF

½ C butter
1 t minced garlic
½ t salt
¼ t black pepper
¼ t sage

¼ t rosemary
¼ t thyme
¼ dry mustard
¼ t tarragon
3 T parsley

Chop all herbs & mix well. Spread on thin slices of rye bread. Reassemble loaf; wrap in foil & heat.

CRAB HUSH PUPPIES

1½ C crab meat
1 T diced onion
1 T diced celery
1 T diced bell pepper
1 T worcestershire sauce

12 crackers
¼ t salt
1 ¼ t pepper
1 C Bisquick
½ C water

Blend crab, vegetables, crushed crackers & seasonings & form into egg size balls. Mix Bisquick with water to form a stiff batter. Roll each ball in batter & drop in 2" hot oil. Turn to brown; remove & drain on a towel. Serves 4-5.

To make herb croutons; Melt 1 T butter & add ¼ t marjoram & ¼ t thyme. Add 1 cup toasted bread cubes in pan & turn to coat well over moderate heat. Drain & add to salads, soups & casseroles.

GARLIC CHIVE ROLLS

3¾ - 4⅛ C flour
1 pkg dry yeast
1 C milk
¼ C sugar
3 eggs

¼ C butter
4 T chives
½ t salt
2 t garlic powder

In processor mix 2 C flour, & yeast. In pan, heat milk, sugar, butter, snipped chives, salt, & garlic powder just until warm & butter is almost melted. Add to flour with eggs. Add as much flour as needed to make a stiff dough. Place in a bowl, cover with plastic wrap & let rise 20 minutes. Punch down & divide into 18 portions the size of an egg. Place in 18 greased muffin tins, cover & let rise until nearly double (20-25 minutes). Bake at 375° for 10 minutes. Makes 18.

SWEET POTATO GINGER ROLLS

1 env dry yeast
2 T sugar
2 T dry milk powder
1 T grated gingerroot
1 t grated orange rind
½ t salt

½ t nutmeg
2 T butter
¾ C sweet potato
3½ C flour
1 egg
sesame seeds

Dissolve yeast in ¼ C warm water. Add sugar & milk to mixture with herbs & spices. Whip butter into cooked mashed potatoes & add to yeast mixture. Add flour & stir to blend. Cover bowl & let rise until double - about 45 minutes. Punch down. Knead lightly on floured board. Pull off pieces of dough the size of ping pong balls & arrange on greased sheet side by side. Let rise 30 minutes. Paint with beaten egg & sprinkle with sesame seeds. Bake at 375° for 12-15 minutes. Makes 36 rolls.

MEDITERRANEAN SPOON BREAD

2 C milk
¾ C yellow cornmeal
2 T butter
½ C stuffed green olives
1 C Muenster cheese

1 T baking powder
1 t salt
1 T sugar
3 eggs

Heat milk with cornmeal to boiling, stirring constantly. Add butter & sliced olives. Simmer for 10 minutes. Remove from heat & stir in cheese. Mix dry ingredients. Beat eggs until light & fluffy & add dry ingredients & cornmeal mixture. Quickly pour into a greased 1½ qt round bowl & bake at 300° for 60 minutes or until top springs back when touched. Serve immediately with butter. Serves 6.

a potpourri of entrees

Potpourri is called the cook's nosegay
Remembrances of the past
Your garden's yield; a prom's corsage
To make scents of ages last.

PASTA WITH GREENS & GARLIC

¼ C olive oil	½ t salt
1 chopped onion	¼ t pepper
3 minced garlic cloves	dash nutmeg
1 lb spinach	1 lb linguine
1 T minced basil	2 T pine nuts

1 C parmesan cheese

Heat oil & saute the onion & garlic until soft. Wash, dry & sliced the spinach into thin shreds & add to oil. Cook just until spinach wilts. Add the herbs & spices. Cook the linguini until done & toss with spinach & nuts. Sprinkle with cheese. Serves 4.

TROPICAL PASTA

1 lb thin spaghetti	2 T olive oil
¼ C sesame seeds	¼ C basil
1 t grated lemon peel	½ t salt
2 T minced parsley	¼ C lemon juice
1 t ground pepper	½ C buttermilk

¾ C shredded unsweetened coconut

Cook pasta until al dente. Drain & toss with remaining ingredients. Serves 6-8.

INTERNATIONAL SPAGHETTI
From the people of the Mediterranean.

¼ lb minced watercress	2 T olive oil
½ C minced basil	3 C spaghetti
2 minced shallots	¼ C pecans

¼ C crumbled feta cheese

Cook the watercress, basil & shallots in oil until just wilted. Cook spaghetti & toss with greens, chopped pecans & cheese. Serves 4.

entrees
85

MICROWAVE FRITTATA

3 chopped green onions   2 T milk
½ lb cut asparagus   2 T mint
3 eggs   Salt & pepper

Place all ingredients in a greased glass pie plate & whisk together well. Cover with vented plastic wrap & microwave until eggs are set - about 8 minutes on medium. Rotate dish midway. Let stand a few minutes before serving. Serves 6.
Variation: Substitute black olives, chopped artichoke hearts, 1 T oregano & 2 T grated provolone cheese for the vegetables & herbs in above recipe.

GUACAMOLE TACOS

1 chopped onion   ⅓ C green onion
2 T oil   2 T lemon juice
16 oz tomatoes   2¼ t cumin
4 oz chopped green chilis 2 garlic cloves
1 t salt   8 taco shells
⅛ t chopped oregano   1½ C lettuce
2 mashed avocados   ¾ C cheese

Saute chopped onion in oil until soft. Add tomatoes, chilis, ½ t salt & oregano & simmer 20 minutes. Combine next 5 ingredients & fill taco shells. Spoon tomato mixture over & sprinkle with lettuce & cheese. Serves 8.

EGG TRICKS

Add 4 chive stems & 12 chive blooms to an omelet just as it is about to set.

Add 1 T chopped parsley, 1 t chopped chives, ¼ t dried tarragon & ⅛ t Tabasco to a 2 egg omelet. Cook as usual.

entrees
86

MAIO'S MAGIC LASAGNA

This magical dish comes from an accomplished lady- besides the kitchens!

6 T butter	1 t oregano
8 T flour	2 C mozzarella
4 C milk	2 C ricotta
2 T olive oil	2 C parmesan
⅔ C minced onion	¼ C tomato sauce
1 C raisins	1 lb lasagna noodles
30 oz frozen spinach	4 bell peppers
1 t nutmeg	½ C warm water
1 t basil	⅔ C pureed pimentos

Make a white sauce with butter, flour & milk, stirring until smooth & thickened. Heat olive oil & saute the onion until soft. Add raisins. Cook & drain the 3 pkgs of spinach & add to onion mixture with the herbs. Add 2½ C white sauce to the spinach & salt & pepper if needed. Shred the mozzarella cheese & mix the three cheeses together. Spread tomato sauce on bottom of a 10x13 pan & cover with the uncooked lasagna noodles. Layer half the spinach mixture on top; then half the pepper strips; half cheese mixture; a layer of noodles. Repeat the layers ending with noodles. Pour the remainder of white sauce on top & ½ C water around edge of dish. Make a border of pureed pimentos around edge of dish. Bake at 350° for 60 minutes until bubbly. Serves 10-12. Freezes well.

SPINACH PIZZA

Cover your favorite pizza crust with 10 oz chopped spinach, drained; 3 t oregano; 2 t basil; 1 C sliced mushrooms & ¾ C grated mozzarella cheese. Bake 425° 25 minutes.

TOMATO PESTO TART

1 baked pastry shell
2 beaten eggs
1 C cottage cheese
1 t basil
½ C plain yogurt
12 cherry tomato

PARSLEY PESTO

1 egg
2 T oil
2 C parsley
2 t basil
1 garlic clove
3 T bread crumbs
¼ C parmesan cheese

Bake the pastry without pricking. Combine eggs, cottage cheese, minced basil & yogurt & pour into pie shell. Cut tomatoes in halves & place cut side up around filling. Bake at 325° for 30 minutes until knife inserted comes clean. Remove from oven. Make the pesto by combining all ingredients in a processor. Puree until smooth. Place a teaspoon in center of each tomato. Serve at room temperature. Serves 6. Chill rest of pesto & use on pasta.

OMELET TRICKS:

PEACH OMELET PANACEA

Heat 4 sliced peaches, pinch of nutmeg, & a pinch of cinnamon. Stir to coat peaches evenly. Serve on any omelet. Serves 4.

APPLE AND HERB CHEESE OMELET

Saute 1 sliced apple with 1 T butter & ½ T sugar. Add 5 eggs on top of apples & cook as for an omelet. Spread soft herb cheese on top of eggs (the heat will melt the cheese). Cut in 4 wedges to serve. Serves 6.

HERB SOUFFLE

4 T butter	1 t tarragon
3 T flour	2 t thyme
½ t salt	¼ C chives
¼ t pepper	¼ C parsley
1 C milk	¼ C dill
5 eggs, separated	¼ C basil
¼ t cream of tartar	1 T parmesan

Melt butter; add the flour, salt, pepper, & bubble for a minute. In another pan, boil the milk; add the flour mixture & whisk until thickened. Add egg yolks one by one while stirring. Add the crushed herbs. Whip the egg whites with cream of tartar until stiff. Gently fold into herb mix. Dust a souffle dish with the parmesan cheese & pour into the greased dish & bake at 375° for 25 minutes. Serve with Sauce.

SAUCE:

½ C sour cream	1 t lemon juice
½ lb chopped tomatoes	¾ t cornstarch

Puree all ingredients in a processor. Heat until thick. Serve with souffle.

FIVE CHEESE PIE

16 oz crescent rolls	8 oz cream cheese
8 oz Monterey Jack	2 beaten eggs
8 oz Muenster Cheese	4 T butter
8 oz Cheddar Cheese	1 garlic clove
8 oz Swiss Cheese	2 t Italian Season P.12
4 T sesame seeds	

Place half the rolls on a 9x13 pan. Press seams together. Slice cheeses & layer on top of crust. Mix all else & pour on cheeses. Top with other rolls pressing seams together. Bake at 350° for 45 min.

entrees
89

VERY VEGETABLE CHILI

2 T olive oil
1 chopped onion
2 minced garlic cloves
2 zucchini, cubed
1 chopped bell pepper
16 oz tomatoes
15 oz kidney beans
2 t ground cumin
2 t dried oregano
2 t dried basil
1 t black pepper
½ t salt
1 t fennel seeds
¼ C parsley
1 T chili powder
¼ C chopped dill
2 T lemon juice
Garnishes

Heat oil & saute onion & garlic until soft. Add vegetables & herbs & cook 30 minutes, uncovered. Add lemon juice & serve immediately. Garnish with sour cream & Monterey Jack cheese.

ARTICHOKE STUFFED CHICKEN

6 boned chicken breasts
12 oz artichoke hearts
1 C Monterey Jack
8 oz cream cheese
8 T butter
1 t Italian seas.p.12
2 garlic cloves
4 eggs
    4 C buttered bread crumbs

Pound breasts ¼" thick. Mix chopped artichokes, grated cheeses, butter & herbs & form into 6 oval logs. Chill. Place one log on the long side of the chicken breast & roll up. Tuck sides in so log is enclosed. Hold rolls together with toothpicks. Mix eggs & dip each roll in egg, then in crumbs. Chill. Bake at 400° for 30 minutes. Serves 6.

BLACKENED HERBS

1 T dried marjoram
1 T dried oregano
1 T dried thyme
1 t salt
1 t pepper
½ t cayenne
    Use on any fish, fowl, or meat.

HERBED TURKEY & STUFFING

10-12 lb turkey
1½ C grated Monterey Jack
3 C diced celery
2 C chopped mushrooms
3 C bread crumbs
10 oz spinach, drained
½ C butter
2 chopped onions
½ t salt
¼ t pepper
1 t rosemary
1 t thyme
1 beaten egg

GLAZE:
¼ C oil
¼ t dried rosemary
3 garlic cloves
¼ t dried thyme

Clean turkey. Make stuffing by combining all the chopped & grated ingredients & heat to melt butter. Stuff turkey or cook separately. Make a glaze & baste the turkey during cooking.

CHICKS WITH ROSEMARY SAUCE

1 C Dijon mustard
1 t minced garlic
1 C honey
2 T rosemary
8 Cornish Game Hens

Blend ingredients together & brush on chickens. Arrange on rack & bake at 425° for 2 hours, brushing with glaze every 15 minutes. Serves 8.

CRANBERRY AND SPICE

12 oz fresh cranberries
½ C sugar
½" sliced gingerroot
2 cinnamon stks
½ C apple cider
2" lemon peel
¼ C ginger ale

Bring all ingredients to a boil & simmer 10 minutes. Chill. When serving, remove spices. Makes 2 cups.

MINT JULEP CHICKEN

1 t lemon pepper
4 boned chicken breasts
2 T oil
¼ C orange juice
¼ C chicken broth

1 T lemon juice
½ t lemon peel
2 T white wine
2 T brown sugar
1 T chopped mint

Sprinkle lemon pepper over skinned chicken. Heat oil in pan & brown chicken on both sides. Drain fat & add juices, broth, peel & wine. Mix well. Spoon sauce over chicken; sprinkle with brown sugar & mint. Cover & cook on low until tender. Serves 4.

YOGURT MARINATED CHICKEN

4 chopped scallions
2 lemons, juiced
4 minced garlic cloves
1 bunch cilantro
2 t chili powder

1 C yogurt
4 jalapeños
2 t grnd cumin
1 t salt
1 t pepper

12 pieces of boned chicken

Combine all ingredients except chicken in a processor & blend smooth. Pour over chicken & coat completely. Chill overnight. Grill or bake at 350° for 60 minutes. Serves 12.

OLIVE HERB TURKEY

1 lb sliced turkey
3 T oil
2 t rosemary

¾ C white wine
2 t basil
½ C ripe olives

Saute turkey in oil until brown. Remove from pan & add all else to pan drippings. Cook briefly until thickened. Serve over turkey slices. Serves 4.

entrees
92

CHICKEN MOUSSE WITH PARSLEY

2 chicken halves	½ t salt
2 T parsley	¼ t pepper
4 green onions	1½ C cream
3 T lemon juice	1 T butter

CILANTRO SAUCE:

2 C chicken stock	⅛ t pepper
4 t lemon juice	3 T parsley
¼ C butter	

Process the chicken, parsley, onions, juice, salt & pepper & cream until smooth. Butter small timbale cups & fill with ½ C chicken mixture. Bake at 325° for 20-25 minutes until knife in center comes clean. Make the sauce by boiling the stock until reduced to 1 cup. Add the remaining ingredients & serve over the unmolded chicken mousse. Serves 6.

DILL CHICKEN

8 chicken breasts	1 C sour cream
2 T sherry wine	1 T flour
1 T currant jelly	2 T dill seeds
½ t tomato paste	1 C stock
1 T parmesan cheese	salt & pepper

Brown chicken in a pan & add sherry. Remove chicken & add remainder of ingredients. Return chicken to pan & cook 20-30 minutes. Pour the sauce over & brown in oven.

DILL SAUCE:

2 C mushrooms	1 T sherry
2 T dill weed	4 T butter

Saute all in pan & serve with chicken. Serves 8.

PEPPERCORN CHICKEN

½ C olive oil
1 T chopped parsley
1 T chopped basil
1 T chopped thyme
1 garlic clove
4 chicken breasts
2 T apple jelly
2 T peppercorns
¼ C white wine

Mix first 5 ingredients together. Debone chicken & dip in herb oil to coat well. Grill or broil 4" from heat 8-10 minutes until cooked & juices run clear. Bring jelly, green peppercorns & wine to a boil for 1 minute & pour over chicken. Serves 4.

CHICKEN CHEESE ROLLS

1 ½ T olive oil
1 ½ C chopped onion
3 minced garlic cloves
4 chopped tomatoes
½ C white wine
½ C parsley
2 t oregano
½ t pepper
24 oz chicken
4 oz feta cheese
6 crusty sandwich rolls

Heat oil & saute onion & garlic for 5 minutes. Add tomatoes, wine & herbs & cook 20 minutes until thickened. Cut chicken into bite size pieces & cook with tomatoes for 15 minutes. Add cheese & cook 10 more minutes. Chill & serve on rolls. Serves 6.

HERBS FOR OVEN FRIED CHICKEN

½ C Italian bread crumbs
2 t curry powder
2 t onion powder
¾ t salt
dash red pepper
¼ t garlic powder

Dip chicken pieces in milk & roll in herbed crumbs. Bake at 375° for 50 minutes until done.

OREGANO PORK MEXICANA

2 lb pork tenderloin
1 clove garlic
½ t oregano
3 T oil
½ C chopped ripe olives
½ C raisins
½ C bell pepper
1 C chili sauce
¼ t cayenne
2 T flour
2 C water
½ t cumin seed

Rub tenderloin with crushed garlic and oregano. Brown in oil & add olives, raisins, chopped pepper, chili sauce & cayenne pepper. Mix flour in ¾ C water & stir into pan gently. Add remaining water & stir until smooth. Bake at 350° for 30 minutes or until done. Before serving sprinkle generously with cumin seed. Serves 4 - 6.

VARIATION: Insert garlic slivers in meat & rub with 3 t salt, ¼ t pepper, 1 T dried rosemary & ½ t ground cumin.

BLACK FOREST PORK CHOPS

4 pork chops
2 T oil
¼ C beef stock
16oz dark pitted cherries
½ t grated lemon rind
2 T lemon juice
½ t nutmeg
½ t grnd cloves
½ t marjoram
2 t cornstarch
½ C toasted walnuts

Trim fat from pork chops & cook in oil until brown. Drain fat; add stock & simmer 1 hour. Meanwhile drain syrup from cherries & add lemon rind, juice & herbs. Mix a little syrup with the cornstarch & slowly add to rest of syrup. Cook on low until thick & glossy. Pour syrup over chops the last 15 minutes of cooking. Add cherries & chopped walnuts & warm through. Serves 4.

entrees
95

PORK CHOPS WITH DILL SAUCE

2 T butter
4 pork chops
¼ t garlic powder
½ t dill weed
¼ t caraway seed
¼ t paprika
⅛ t salt
2 sliced onions
1 C water
½ C yogurt

Heat butter & brown pork chops. Pour out grease & add all ingredients except yogurt. Cover & simmer for 1 hour - add more water if necessary. Remove pork chops; add yogurt & warm. Pour over chops to serve. Serves 4.
Substitute fennel seed for the dill & caraway seed.

SAGE WRAPPED PORK TENDERLOINS

2 lbs pork tenderloins
2 T Dijon mustard
1 C bread crumbs
2 t sage
1 garlic clove
⅛ t pepper

Trim tenderloins & brush with the mustard. Mix all remaining ingredients until blended. Sprinkle bread crumb mixture over pork. Bake at 400° for 30 minutes until done. Serves 4.

GINGERED PORK

1 C plain yogurt
1 T minced gingerroot
1 t grt orange rind
¼ t salt
¼ t red pepper
2 t coriander
2 pork tenderloins

Mix all ingredients except pork until blended. Marinate pork in mixture overnight turning often to coat well. Remove pork from marinade & reserve mixture. Bake at 400° for 30 minutes, basting with reserved marinade every 15 minutes. Serves 4.

GINGERED HAMBURGERS

1 ½ lb ground beef	1 t soy sauce
½ C chopped scallions	¼ t pepper
¼ C chicken stock	1 t garlic
2 t grated gingerroot	½ C crumbs

Put the pork or beef in a bowl & blend in all other ingredients. Divide mixture into 8 patties 1" thick. Cook in pan until done. Serve with Tomato Sauce. Serves 8.

TOMATO SAUCE:

1 T olive oil	½ t dried thyme
¼ C chopped onions	½ t salt
2 C chopped tomatoes	1 bay leaf
1 T chopped garlic	¼ t pepper
2 T chopped basil	

Heat oil & saute onions until wilted. Add all except basil & cook 20 minutes. Remove bay leaf & add basil just before serving.

MEAT LOAF EXTRORDINAIRE

2 lbs ground beef	2 beaten eggs
1 ¼ C bread crumbs	1 chopped onion
2 C chopped parsley	1 t pepper
1 minced garlic clove	¼ t grn allspice
2 T chopped bell pepper	⅛ t nutmeg
⅛ t red pepper	1 T thyme
3 bay leaves	

Combine all ingredients except bay leaves & mix lightly. Put in 2 qt casserole & arrange bay leaves on top. Bake at 350° for 1 hour. Drain fat. Serves 8.

CROCKED HAM

1 lb country ham
1 T tarragon vinegar
1 t dried thyme
3 garlic cloves
¾ C soft butter
1 T cognac

Combine all ingredients in a processor. Puree until smooth. Chill in 3 one cup crocks & smooth top. Serves 6.

LITTLE LAMB TRICKS

2 T Dijon mustard
2 t chopped thyme
¼ t pepper
1 t oregano
8 lamb chops

Smear herb mixture on each chop & grill or broil until done.

MARINADE:
1 t fennel seeds
2 t coriander seeds
2 cardamon pods
1 t snipped lemon grass
2 C oil
1 sliced onion
2 whole allspice
1 lemon, sliced

Marinate 1½ lb lamb cubes in the marinade overnight. Make into kabobs & grill.

AROMATIC LEG OF LAMB

7 lb leg of lamb
1½ T minced mint
1 T minced oregano
½ t cinnamon
½ t salt
¼ t pepper
¼ t nutmeg
⅓ C lemon juice
2 crushed garlic cloves

Trim fat from lamb & brush with all the ingredients mixed together. Place lamb on a rack & bake uncovered at 325° until meat thermometer reaches 150° for medium. Remove from oven and let stand 15 minutes. Slice across grain into 16 thin slices.

entrees

FRUITED SALMON

1 ½ lb salmon fillets
1 lb seedless grapes
salt & pepper
3 T olive oil
½ C white wine
1 minced onion
1 t curry powder
1 T flour
1 T candy ginger
1 C stock
¼ C cream

Cut fillets into 4 pieces. Cut grapes in half. Season salmon with salt & pepper & put in 1 T oil in dish with wine. Cover & bake at 400° for 20 minutes until cooked. Melt remaining oil & saute onion. Add curry, flour, chopped candied ginger & cook 10 seconds. Remove from heat & stir in fish or chicken stock & cream. Bring to a boil & simmer until 1 cup remains. Stir in grapes & spoon over salmon. Serves 4.

FLOUNDER STUFFED

10 oz chopped spinach
2 T oil
½ C chopped mushrooms
¼ C chopped onion
1 minced garlic clove
½ C bread crumbs
¼ C feta cheese
⅛ t pepper
4 flounder fillets
2 T white wine

Cook spinach according to directions & drain well. Heat oil & cook mushrooms, onion & garlic until mushrooms release their juices. Add to spinach with crumbs, cheese & pepper. Place 3 T stuffing on flounder & roll up. Spoon remaining stuffing in greased dish & place flounder rolls on top. Spoon wine over. Cover. Bake at 375° for 20 minutes until done. Uncover for last 5 minutes. Serves 4.

entrees
99

WHITE FISH ROLLS ON VEGETABLES

½ lb snow peas
4 slivered carrots
⅛ t pepper
1 lb fish fillets
8 slices gingerroot

4 scallions
1 t oil
1 T orange peel
1 t garlic
2½ T soy sauce

In a steam basket, place snow peas & carrots & sprinkle with pepper. Roll fish fillets loosely & place on top with gingerroot & sliced scallions. Cover & steam 8 minutes. Make a sauce by heating the oil & adding orange peel & minced garlic & heating 1 minute. Add soy sauce & 3 T water & bring to a boil. Pour sauce over vegetables & serve. Serves 4.

BAKED OYSTERS IN FENNEL SAUCE

1 chopped fennel bulb
¼ lb sliced mushrooms
¼ C white wine
⅓ C water
4 turns pepper mill

24 oysters in shells
4 T butter
¼ C dill
1 T Pernod

Prepare sauce by combining fennel, mushrooms, wine, water & pepper; cover & simmer for 8 minutes. Puree all in a processor until smooth. Scrub the oyster shells & place in a pan in a single layer. Bake at 500° for 7 minutes just until oysters pop open. Remove the top shell with a knife. Pour the juice of a few oysters into the sauce being sure not to make it too runny. Mix the sauce with the butter, chopped dill & Pernod. Heat to boiling & spoon over oysters in half shell. Serves 6.

Yarrow under pillows would bestow the vision of future lovers.

entrees
100

MINTED THREADED SHRIMP

1 t chili powder	1 T vinegar
1 minced garlic clove	¼ t pepper
1 T chopped mint	1 t salt
1 t chopped basil	¾ C oil

2 lb raw shrimp shelled

Add all ingredients together & marinate overnight in the refrigerator. Thread on skewers & grill or broil in oven, basting well. Serves 10.

CRAB BOAT TANDOORI

6 oz plain yogurt	4 cucumbers
1 lemon. juiced	3 beaten eggs
4 t tandoori or curry	4 T butter
1½ C bread crumbs	1 lb crabmeat
2 t dill weed	2 green onions
⅛ t cayenne pepper	½ green pepper

Combine yogurt, lemon juice & 3 t tandoori or curry powder. Set aside. Mix crumbs, dill & cayenne. Peel cucumbers & slit lengthwise; scoop out seeds; dip in eggs & crumbs. Deep fry in hot oil until brown. Drain. Melt butter & add 1 t tandoori & crab. Saute 3 minutes with chopped onions & chopped pepper. Blend in yogurt. Fill cucumber boats with crab & heat for 2 minutes. Serves 8.

SHRIMP MARINADE

Marinate shrimp in olive oil, wine, Dijon mustard & fresh basil. Wrap 24 shrimp in large basil leaves & prosciutto ham. Grill.

Witches of old connected the violets with its ability to provide sound sleep.

HOT STUFFED AVOCADOS

3 avocados	½ t salt
6 T vinegar	dash pepper
6 slices garlic	1 T grated onion
2 T butter	¼ t celery salt
2 T flour	2 C crab meat
1 C cream	dash of cayenne
½ t worcestershire sauce	¼ C sharp cheese

Cut avocados in half & remove pit & put 1 T vinegar & 1 garlic sliver in each half. Let stand 30 minutes. Make a sauce with the remaining ingredients except cheese & cook until thickened. Pour vinegar & garlic from avocados & fill with creamed mixture. Grate the cheese & sprinkle over avocados. Bake at 350° for 15 minutes until cheese melts. Serves 6.

COLD MINT SAUCE FOR FISH

1 C cottage cheese	½ C parsley
1 garlic clove	¼ C mint

Blend all ingredients in a processor until smooth. Use in place of tartar sauce with fish. Makes 1½ cups.

MARBLED EGGS IN A NEST

10 eggs	4 T oil
6 strong teabags	1 T vinegar
8 oz green linguine	salt & pepper
8 oz white linguine	1 T basil
1 C ham strips	1 garlic clove

Cook eggs in boiling water for 1 minute. Remove & crack shell all over. Add teabags to water & return eggs; cook 1 minute. Leave to cool. Cook linguine & add all else. Toss. Make nests & add shelled eggs.

entrees
102

SANDWICHES

ZUCCHINI FILLING:

4 shredded zucchini	1 t sugar
8 oz plain yogurt	1 t basil
¼ C sliced scallions	½ t salt

Press zucchini to remove water. Add remaining ingredients & mix well. Chill. Spread on rye bread for an open faced sandwich. Makes 12.

RAISIN BREAD SURPRISE:

1 chopped apple	1 C celery
1 C grated carrots	1 C sharp cheese
2 sliced scallions	1 C raisins
½ t cinnamon	¼ t ginger

10 slices raisin bread

Chop or grate all the ingredients except bread & mix well. Spread on raisin bread for closed or open faced sandwiches.

ESTELLE'S HERB SANDWICHES:
These never failed to make a hit at her garden tea parties.

1 C any green herb   1 onion
½ C mayonnaise

Mix the minced herbs with the grated onion & just enough mayonnaise to moisten. Spread sparsely on thin sliced bread.

As aromatic plants bestow
No spicy fragrance while they grow;
But crush'd or trodden to the ground,
Diffuse their balmy sweets around.
Oliver Goldsmith

These sorbets are to cleanse the palate between courses.

LEMON & BAY LEAF GRANITA

1 C water
6 bay leaves
¼ C sugar

2 C sweet wine
1 C lemon juice
¼ C lime juice

Bring water & bay leaves to a boil for 3 minutes. Add sugar to water & stir until dissolved. Cool completely. Remove bay leaves. Mix all remaining ingredients & freeze in a covered container, stirring occasionally. Serve in bowls. Makes 6 cups.

HONEY AND MINT ICE

1 ½ C cold water
½ C ginger mint leaves
½ C honey
1 C orange juice
1 t grated orange peel

½ t cinnamon
pinch of salt
2 T lemon juice
1 C heavy cream
6 T Cointreau

3 T chopped walnuts

Boil together water, mint & honey for 2 minutes without stirring. Remove from heat & add juices, peel & spices. Strain & freeze in tray or shallow dish. When serving pour Cointreau over ice. If using as a dessert, top with the cream, whipped & chopped walnuts. Makes 4 cups.

TOMATO AND BASIL SORBET

2 lbs peeled tomatoes
1 T sugar

½ t lemon juice
8 basil leaves

Combine all ingredients in a processor. Puree. Freeze in ice cube trays. To serve, process a few cubes in a processor until slushy. Garnish with basil.

entrees

CAPPUCINO GRANITA

½ C water
1 C sugar
3 C expresso coffee
½ t cinnamon
½ C light cream
2 T Kahlua

Bring the water & sugar to a boil & simmer for 5 minutes. Remove from heat & cool. Add remaining ingredients & mix well. Freeze in freezer until solid. Makes 1 qt.

"Lavender is to comfort and dry up the moisture of a cold brain."

MINT SHERBET

3 C water
1 C sugar
1 lemon, grated
4 lemons, juiced
½ C mint leaves
1 C whiskey
2 egg whites
mint springs

Boil together the water & sugar for 5 minutes. Add rind & juice. Steep chopped mint leaves in whiskey for 1 hour. Strain out leaves & add lemon mixture. Pour in freezer & freeze until thick. Whip egg whites until soft peaks form. Fold into slushy mixture. Freeze until hard. Garnish with mint sprigs. Serves 6.

HORSERADISH SHERBET

1 C sour cream
2 T grated horseradish
1 T lemon juice
1 T applesauce
Salt & white pepper to taste

Combine all ingredients in a processor. Puree until smooth. Freeze in shallow tray, stirring occasionally. Serve with a beef or pork dish. Serves 2-4.

a tussie mussie of vegetables

Tussie Mussies are circles of herbs,
Nosegays carried by my daughter;
Rosemary for memories; thyme for a beau;
Sentiments without water.

vegetables

CURRIED ASPARAGUS

1 lb cooked asparagus	2 t curry
1 C mayonnaise	1 t savory
⅛ t chili powder	1 T parsley
½ t worcestershire	½ t salt
1½ t lemon juice	½ C yogurt
1 T chopped green onions	3 t capers

Arrange warm asparagus on a plate. Combine all other ingredients & pour over in an attractive pattern. Makes 1 C mayonnaise.

BROCCOLI CHEWY RICE

3 C cooked rice	½ lb mushrooms
2 T oil	1 green pepper
1 chopped onion	2 lb broccoli
2 minced garlic cloves	½ C cashews
½ t dill	½ lb Gruyere &
2 t thyme	¼ parmesan
1 t oregano	cheeses
½ bunch chopped parsley	1 C yogurt

While rice is cooking, heat oil & saute onion, garlic & herbs. Add the sliced vegetables & stir fry until crisp. As soon as broccoli changes color, add nuts & remove from heat. Spread rice in a 9x13 dish & cover with vegetable mixture, then grated cheeses & yogurt. Bake at 350° for 20 minutes or until bubbly.

Make an herb butter with 4 T butter, 1 T each chopped parsley, chives, dill & 1 t pepper & ¼ C parmesan cheese. Good on asparagus.

CONFETTI VEGETABLES

1 oz shiitake mushrooms
1 C butter
1 T rosemary
4 onions, quartered
2 C broccoli
6 carrots
2 bell peppers
(red & green)

Soak mushrooms in hot water for 15 minutes. Drain & reserve liquid. Cream butter & mushrooms & 1 T reserved liquid until smooth. Cook vegetables in the reserved water with rosemary until just tender. Just before serving add butter & toss to coat well. Add salt & pepper if necessary. Serves 8.

BASIL BEANS

1 lb green beans
½ C toasted almonds
¼ C olive oil
¼ C vinegar
1 T oregano
½ t basil
½ t garlic salt
¼ t salt
¼ pepper
¼ C parmesan

Cook beans until barely tender; chill. Heat with all ingredients except cheese until beans are well cooked. Serve with Parmesan cheese sprinkled on top. May be served cold.

SESAME GREEN BEANS

1 lb green beans
1 T toasted sesame seeds
1 t oil
1 t lemon peel

Cook green beans until tender. Drain & toss with remaining ingredients. Serves 4.

vegetables

ST PATRICK'S BEANS

4 oz green chilis	1 green onion
1 bunch parsley	1 garlic clove
2 T plain yogurt	½ lime, juiced
4 turns pepper mill	1 lb green beans

Puree all ingredients in a processor except beans. Cook beans until just tender. Pour dressing over beans. Serve hot or cold. Serves 4.

RED, WHITE & HERBED

¼ C butter	2 onions
2 T oil	2 garlic cloves
1 lb green beans	1 t salt
1 lb fennel bulb	2 t basil
2 bell peppers	¼ t pepper

Heat butter & oil & add all the ingredients & mix well. Cook 15 minutes, stirring occasionally until vegetables are tender. Serves 8.

SOUR CREAM EGGPLANT

1 small eggplant	¼ t chili
3 T butter	1 C sour cream
	¼ t garlic salt

Peel eggplant & cut into ¼" cubes. Heat butter & saute eggplant until soft & golden. Remove from heat. Add remaining ingredients & mix well; pour over eggplant. Toss lightly & chill before serving. Serve with curry dishes.

Mexicans drink garlic tea to cure the pain of arthritis & rub raw garlic on fingernails to prevent chipping.

BABY VEGETABLES PICKS

4 bunches baby turnips
4 bunches baby carrots
4 bunches baby beets
3 C chicken stock
1 bouquet garni

3 C wine
1 ½ C milk
⅓ C olive oil
pepper to taste
4 T parsley

Wash & trim vegetables & set aside by vegetable group. Heat broth, bouquet garni & wine to boiling. Add vegetables & cook until just tender. Make a marinade of the remaining ingredients. Place vegetables in a pattern on skewers & marinate 4 hours. Grill, basting often with marinade.

SOUTHERN COLLARD GREENS & DUMPLINGS

4 lbs collard greens
DUMPLINGS:
¾ C cornmeal
½ C flour
½ C Monterey Jack
1 t baking powder
1 t nutmeg

1 lb pork bones

¼ t salt
¼ C scallions
1 T sugar
1 egg
Vinegar

Cook the greens in just enough water to cover & add the pork bones. Bring to a boil & simmer, covered 25 minutes until greens are soft. Uncover & reduce liquid by ⅓. Make the dumplings by mixing all ingredients except egg & vinegar until blended. Make a well in the center & add the beaten egg & ½ C broth from the cooked greens. Mix just to blend. Drop heaping tablespoons of the batter on the simmering greens, keeping the dumplings several inches apart. Cover & simmer for 12 minutes. Uncover & cook 5 minutes more or until dumplings are dry on top. Serve with vinegar. Serves 6.

CABBAGE FOR OUTDOORS

one half head cabbage	¼ t salt
2 sliced onions	¼ t pepper
2 tomatoes, chopped	1 bouillon cube
1 t Italian season-p.12	2 green peppers

Chop vegetables coarsely. Mix all ingredients on a piece of foil & close tightly. Bake at 350° for 60 minutes until soft. Can be cooked on a grill or in a smoker. Serves 8.

SOUTH SEA ISLAND CABBAGE

¼ C butter	1 cabbage
1 T mustard seeds	½ -1 C coconut
1 sliced onion	½ t salt
¼ C sliced green pepper	⅛ t pepper
	2 t curry powder

Heat butter & stir in mustard seeds until they sputter. Add onion & green pepper & stir fry 10 minutes. Add the sliced cabbage, coconut & the spices; cover & steam 5 minutes. Toss lightly & steam 10 more minutes. Toss & serve. Serves 6.

Herbs are for present joys, for present beauty. Herbs are for memories of long ago. And herbs are hopes for the future. My little grandaughter & grandson walk with me among my herbs & we smell & talk together about "fairies resting in beds of thyme", Cinderella in her pumpkin coach & I tell them about their mother years ago on sunny summer days doing the same thing. I have great hopes & almost now know something of the peace, the fragrance, the joy of today & of yesterday will pass down the years, by way of the herb garden, to these children of today & to all the children of the future. Mother's Journal

vegetables
111

GARLIC LOVERS MUSHROOMS

8 unpeeled garlic cloves
1 lb mushrooms
1 t thyme
¼ C butter

4 garlic cloves
2 T olive oil
2 T wine vinegar
salt & pepper

Prick the unpeeled garlic with a knife & bake at 350° for 30 minutes. Peel garlic & spread with mushrooms in 1 layer in a dish. Add snipped thyme. Mash butter & 4 minced garlic cloves & spoon over the mushrooms & garlic cloves. Drizzle with the remaining ingredients. Bake at 450° for 20 minutes. Serve with French bread to mop up the essence. Serves 4.

CARAMELIZED ONIONS

6 onions
¼ C olive oil
1 t garlic
3 turns pepper mill

1 T parsley
¼ C water
1 t vinegar
½ t salt

pinch of red pepper

Cut stem & root ends off of onions. Slice ¾" leaving skin on. Place on greased baking sheet & brush with oil. Bake at 300° for 1 ½ hours turning over partway through cooking. Place in flat dish & remove skin. Combine remaining ingredients & pour over onions. Cover & let marinate for at least 2 hours. Serve at room temperature. Serves 6.

Southernwood was also called Lad's Love because its ashes were rubbed on faces of boys to make their beards grow.

SOUSED ONIONS

¼ C raisins	4 t brown sugar
¼ C bourbon	3 tomatoes
4 onions, quartered	¼ t salt
3 T oil	sprig of thyme
½ t black pepper	

Soak raisins in bourbon. Peel & quarter onions & saute in oil for 5 minutes. Sprinkle brown sugar over & cook 5 minutes on low. Add chopped tomatoes & salt & cook 5 minutes more. Add raisins, bourbon, thyme & pepper. Pour into a dish, cover & bake at 350° for 60 minutes. Cool & serve at room temperature. Serves 6.

THOUSAND HERB POTATOES

6 cooked potatoes	1 C milk
1 minced onion	½ t basil
¼ t poultry seasoning	½ t oregano
1 C chopped celery	¼ C parsley
½ t rosemary	2 t salt
¼ t black pepper	½ t thyme
5 T melted margarine	

Cut cooked potatoes in half lengthwise, scoop out potatoes, preserving shells. Mash potatoes; add remaining ingredients & mix well. Fill shells with mixture. Bake at 400° for 20 minutes until top is golden. Serves 6.

ROSEMARY POTATOES

Boil small balls of baking potatoes (cut with a melon baller) with sprigs of rosemary until the potatoes are just crisp tender. Saute them in very hot oil & brown. Sprinkle with chopped rosemary.

FENNEL POTATOES

5 cooked potatoes
2 t chopped fennel leaves
 or 1 T fennel seeds
4 T butter
1 egg
¼ C milk
⅛ t paprika
salt & pepper

Mash peeled cooked potatoes & stir in fennel & 2 T butter. Mix the remaining butter, egg & milk. Place potatoes in a greased dish; spread egg/milk mixture over top. Sprinkle with salt & pepper to taste & paprika on top. Bake at 350° 30 minutes. Serves 6.

YELLOWED YOGURT POTATOES

1 chopped onion
1 T olive oil
4 oz green chilis
½ t tumeric
½ t curry powder
½ t cumin
pinch of salt
⅛ t pepper
3 T balsamic
 vinegar
½ C cilantro
1½ C yogurt
12 cooked new potatoes

Saute onion in oil until brown. Add chopped chilis, spices, salt & pepper & cook 5 minutes. Remove from heat, add vinegar, chopped cilantro & let cool. Stir in plain yogurt & potatoes with a wooden spoon to avoid breaking up. Serve warm or cold. Serves 4.

POTATOES GARLIC FRIED

5 potatoes
¼ C oil
¼ C butter
4 garlic cloves

Peel potatoes & cut in chunks. Heat oil & butter & add potatoes in a single layer. Cook for 5 minutes. Add minced garlic & cook 20 more minutes until brown & crisp. Drain. Serves 4.

PARSLEY RICE LOAF

3 C cooked rice	1 t salt
1 C chopped parsley	3 eggs
⅓ C chopped onion	1½ C milk
¾ C shredded sharp cheese	

Mix rice, parsley, onion & salt. Combine eggs, milk & cheese & add rice. Pour into a greased loaf pan & bake at 325° for 40 minutes. Serves 4-6.

SPICY MINT RICE

This combination is lovely as well as tasty.

1 C cashews	3 C hot water
3 T oil	1 t salt
¼ C raisins	10 oz peas
1½ C raw rice	2 T lime juice
¼ C chopped mint leaves	

Saute cashews in oil; add raisins, rice, water & salt. Simmer covered for 10 minutes. Bake at 350° for 45 minutes. Remove from oven. Stir in peas; let stand covered for 5 minutes. Add juice & mint. Serves 4-6.

AVOCADO RICE BOATS

1 C cooked rice	1 tomato
¼ t ground cumin	¼ C cashews
4 pitted ripe olives	2 avocados
¼ C Italian Dressing	

Cook rice & add cumin & sliced olives. Chopped tomato & cashews & add to rice. Cut avocados & brush with salad dressing. Stuff with rice & heat through. Serves 4.

DILLY RICE

1 T grated lemon peel
1 t minced onion
4 bouillon cubes
2 t dill
1 t salt
2 C raw rice

Mix all together & store. Use as needed. Cook as you would plain rice.

SWEET POTATO CARROT TOSS

1 grated sweet potato
3 grated carrots
1 C grated apple
1 T lemon juice
¼ C butter
⅓ C apple cider
¼ C prunes
3 T raisins
1 T sugar
1 t lemon peel
½ t cinnamon
½ t salt
½ C toasted bread crumbs

Combine grated sweet potato, carrots & apples & sprinkle with lemon juice. Melt butter; add vegetables & cook 8 minutes. Add remaining ingredients except for crumbs & simmer covered for 15 minutes or until tender. Place crumbs in center of vegetables leaving ½" border. Broil 2" from heat for 30-60 seconds until browned. Sprinkle with parsley. Serves 6.

TANGY TOMATO SOUFFLE

3 slices toasted bread
¼ C melted butter
15 oz tomato puree
½ C brown sugar
¼ t cloves
½ t cinnamon

Cube bread; place in baking dish & pour butter over. Boil all else together & pour over bread. Bake at 350° for 45 minutes.

SWEET POTATO CAKES

2 C sweet potatoes
½ C chopped onions
1 t curry powder
¼ t cayenne pepper
½ t black pepper

2 eggs
4 t flour
1 t nutmeg
½ t salt
¼ C oil

Cook & mash sweet potatoes. Add remaining ingredients except oil & mix well. Chill. When ready to serve heat oil & cook by spoonfuls on a griddle. Serve with syrup or applesauce. Makes 12.

SNOW PEAS & GARLIC MEDLEY

¾ lb snow peas
4 bell peppers
¼ C soy sauce
1 T minced garlic
1½ T wine vinegar

1½ T sugar
2 T water
2 t sesame oil
1 t red pepper

String the snow peas & cut peppers into shreds. Add remaining ingredients & mix well. Toss in a pan on high for 2 minutes or until vegetables are still crisp. Serve at room temperature. Serves 6.

SPINACH YOGURT

1 lb spinach
3 T chopped basil
2 T chopped thyme
3 sliced onions

2 T butter
¼ t cinnamon
pinch tumeric
1 C yogurt

Wash spinach & cook for about 3 minutes with water that clings to the leaves. Drain & chop. Saute basil, thyme & onions in butter. Add remaining ingredients & mix well. Serve at room temperature. Serves 4.

HOT STUFF TOMATOES

8 tomatoes	1 t chives
6 oz artichoke hearts	1 garlic clove
1 C mayonnaise	¼ t soy sauce
1 C parmesan cheese	⅛ t red pepper
2 t chopped parsley	pinch pepper

Cut tomatoes in half & scoop out seeds. Drain. Combine all ingredients; spoon 1 T mixture in each tomato shell. Bake at 375° for 20 minutes until bubbly. Serves 4-6.

STUFFED TOMATOES WITH BASIL SAUCE

1 chopped onion	1 C mushrooms
1 minced garlic clove	2 C cooked rice
1 T oil	4 tomatoes
10 basil leaves	¼ C parmesan

Cook first 5 ingredients until chopped mushrooms just begin to exude their juices. Add rice & stuffed hollowed out tomatoes. Top with parmesan cheese & broil until cheese browns. Serve with Dressing.

Dressing:

1 minced garlic clove	1 T lemon juice
12 basil leaves	3 T vinegar
½ C olive oil	

Mix ingredients together & serve over tomatoes. Serves 4.

QUICK HERB TRICKS WITH VEGETABLES

Tomatoes - ½ t sage, ¼ t onion salt
Green Peas - ¼ t sage, ¼ t tarragon
Lima Beans - ¼ t marjoram
Baked Potatoes - ¼ t thyme
Rice - ¼ t savory, ¼ t onion salt
Cabbage - ¼ t basil, ¼ t onion salt

vegetables

MINTED WHEAT TOMATOES

John Denver says "ain't nothin as good as old fashion lovin' & HOME GROWN TOMATOES."

½ C bulgur wheat	1 T vinegar
3 halved tomatoes	1 T olive oil
¼ C chopped onion	¼ t salt
2 T chopped mint leaves	⅛ t pepper
1 T chopped parsley	Mint garnish

Cover bulgur with 1 C water & let sit for 1 hour until grains are plump. Drain. Scoop out tomatoes & chop pulp with onion & herbs & liquids & bulgur. Season to taste. Stuff tomato halves; garnish with extra mint. Serves 6.

ZUCCHINI CAKES WITH ROSEMARY SAUCE

2 eggs, separated	½ t oregano
½ t salt	2 T flour
½ t basil	2 zucchini

Beat eggs separately with ¼ t salt each added to yolks & whites. Fold whites gently into yolks. Add herbs & flour into eggs along with coarsely chopped zucchini. Drop spoonfuls into oil making as flat as possible. Fry on both sides until brown. Remove & serve with Rosemary Sauce. Serves 4-6.

Rosemary Sauce:

1 sliced onion	¼ t rosemary
2 T oil	½ t basil
2 chopped tomatoes	2 C water
	3 T cornstarch

In same pan cook onions in oil. Add tomatoes & herbs. Cook 5 minutes. Thicken with water & cornstarch mixed. Serve over zucchini.

ZESTY ZUCCHINI

3 grated zucchini
3 eggs
6 chopped scallions
½ C chopped mint
½ C chopped parsley

½ C feta cheese
½ C mild cheese
½ C flour
pinch of salt &
 cayenne pepper

Add all ingredients & mix well. Pour into a 9" greased pan & bake at 450° for 45 minutes. Cut into squares. Serve hot or cold. Serves 6-8.

MEXICAN FIESTA SQUASH

3 yellow squash
2 chopped garlic cloves
¼ C chopped onion
¼ C green pepper
4 oz green chilis
1 T olive oil
3 oz Monterey Jack

1 t chili powder
¼ t salt
¼ t pepper
3 T yogurt
2 T taco sauce
2 T cheese
1 T ripe olives

Cook whole squash in water until tender but firm. Cut in half lengthwise & scoop out shells. Cook the chopped pulp, onion, green pepper & chilis in oil until liquid has been absorbed. Remove from heat. Add shredded Monterey Jack cheese & seasonings & yogurt & stuff shells. Bake at 350° for 30 minutes. Divide sauce, shredded Cheddar cheese & sliced olives evenly over squash. Cook 5 more minutes. Serves 6.

HERBED SQUASH

Arrange 8 yellow & green squash in pan with butter & water, ¼ t salt & 1 t rosemary & 1 t thyme. Cook 15 minutes or until tender. Serves 4.

vegetables

THAI VEGETABLES AMERICAN STYLE

1 qt vinegar	3 C sugar
2 blades lemon grass	3 garlic cloves
1 T gingerroot	3 jalapeños

Boil vinegar with herbs & sugar for 5 minutes. Steep for 1 hour.

Vegetables:

4 sliced cucumbers	2 bell peppers
1 bunch scallions	1 grated carrot
1 T cilantro	8 mushrooms

Cut all vegetables into bite size pieces. Add chopped cilantro & marinate in the vinegar solution overnight. Serves 6.

SPICY DRUNKEN FRUIT

1 lb purple plums	4 lemon slices
8 oz peach slices	3 whole cloves
8 oz pear halves	3 whole allspice
8 oz apricot halves	½ t grnd ginger
2 cinnamon sticks	⅓ C port wine

Drain syrup from canned fruit & bring to a boil with the lemon & spices. Reduce heat & simmer 20 minutes. Add the port to syrup & pour over fruits. Let marinate overnight. Heat before serving. Serves 6.

FABULOUS FENNEL

Use fennel as you would celery - it taste like licorice. Use bulb raw in salad or the leaves in stuffings or with pork. Slice fennel in a vegetarian pasta sauce.

a topiary of desserts and pies

A standard of herbs for decor & decorum
The symbols that ruled my life
Lavender for swooning; basil was holy
And chamomile took away strife.

desserts and pies

GINGER PUMPKIN MOUSSE

4 eggs	¾ t cinnamon
7 T sugar	½ t gingerroot
1 T unflavored gelatin	¼ t nutmeg
1½ C pumpkin puree	1 C cream

minced candied ginger garnish

Beat eggs with sugar until light. Add gelatin, pumpkin & spices & grated gingerroot & mix well. Whip cream until soft peaks form. Fold into pumpkin mixture & chill until set. Garnish with chopped candied ginger. Serves 4-6.

PUMPKIN CAKE DESSERT

1 box yellow cake mix	1 t cinnamon
½ C melted butter	½ t ginger
1 egg	½ t grnd cloves
2 C pumpkin	½ t nutmeg
1⅔ C evaporated milk	**Topping:**
½ C sugar	¼ C sugar
½ t salt	½ t cinnamon
2 eggs	3 T butter

Mix cake mix (reserve 1 C for topping), melted butter & egg. Pour into a greased 9x13 pan. Mix next 9 ingredients & pour on top of crust. Make a topping by combining reserved cake mix, sugar, cinnamon and butter. Sprinkle on top & bake at 350° for 50 minutes. Serve with whipped cream. Serves 16.

If you would be at all times merry, eat saffron in meat or drink, & you will never be sad; but beware of eating overmuch, lest you should die of excessive joy.   *Welsh Physicians*

desserts and pies

SWEET GEORGIA BREAD

1 C hot cooked grits
¾ C self rising corn bread
¾ C brown sugar
½ C chopped pecans
¼ t nutmeg

1 C milk
2 T butter
3 beaten eggs
1 t cinnamon
whipped cream

Blend hot grits with all ingredients except whipped cream & stir until butter is melted. Pour into a greased 1½ qt casserole & bake at 350° for 55 minutes or until knife inserted comes out clean. Serve warm with sweet whipped cream. Serves 6.

GEORGE WASHINGTON'S BROWNIE

22 oz cherry pie filling
2 T lemon juice
2 oz unsweet chocolate
6 T butter
¼ C milk
¼ t peppermint extract

2 eggs
1 C sugar
1 C flour
½ t soda
¼ t salt
⅓ C pecans

Mix pie filling & lemon juice & pour in a 2 qt dish. Melt chocolate & butter; stir in milk, extract & eggs. Add dry ingredients & mix well. Chop pecans & fold into batter. Pour evenly over cherry mix. Bake at 350° for 30 minutes until done. Serves 8.

BAY LEAF SAUCE

¼ C brown sugar
2 T flour

6 bay leaves
1 C water
juice of 1 lemon

Combine all; cook for 15 minutes. Remove leaves. Use on puddings, cakes or meats.

desserts and pies

MINT CHOCOLATE MOUSSE

1 pound cake
1 env unflavored gelatin
½ C milk
8 oz cream cheese
½ C sugar
½ t mint extract
green food color
1½ C cream
1 C semisweet chocolate

Cut cake into 16 slices & arrange 4 slices short end down on side of loaf pan & on bottom. Sprinkle gelatin over milk to soften & heat for 2 minutes, stirring until dissolved. Beat cream cheese & sugar & add gelatin. Remove ½ C mixture & add extract & coloring to tint a mint green. Whip cream until soft peaks form. Fold 1 cup into green mixture. Melt chocolate & add to remaining cream cheese with remaining whipped cream. Spoon half of chocolate mixture over cake in bottom of pan. Top with mint mixture; then with chocolate. Chill 3 hours until firm. Serves 12.

COCO-MOCHA MOUSSE

1 env unflavored gelatin
¼ C cold water
15 oz Coco Lopez
¼ C coffee
3 T cocoa
1 t cinnamon
2 C cream, whipped

Sprinkle gelatin over water to soften & heat until dissolved. Combine cream of coconut, cold, strong coffee, unsweetened cocoa & cinnamon & stir in gelatin. Fold in whipped cream. Spoon in parfait glasses & chill until firm. Serves 8.

The English serve small dessert sweets & fruits on lavender sticks.

desserts and pies

CHEERY CHERRY CHEESECAKE

2 C graham cracker crumbs
1½ t cinnamon
½ C melted butter
8 oz cream cheese
1 C ricotta cheese
1 env unflavored gelatin
2 T water
1 T orange juice
1 t strawberry extract
1 C sugar
2 C cherries
1 C cream, whipped

Make crust by combining first 3 ingredients & patting on bottom of a springform pan. Bake at 350° for 10 minutes. Cool. Blend cheeses. Sprinkle gelatin over water & juice to soften & heat until dissolved; add to cheeses with extract & sugar. Blend smooth. Fold in cherries & whipped cream. Pour into crust & chill for 6 hours. Serves 16.

Substitute 1 C eggnog, 4 eggs, ¼ t nutmeg, & 2 T rum for the fruit & cherries in the above recipe for a Christmas Cheesecake.

SPICED HAZELNUT APPLESAUCE SQUARES

1 pkg yellow cake mix
¾ C applesauce
¼ C water
3 eggs
⅓ C oil
1 t cinnamon
½ t mace
2 C chopped hazelnuts

Combine all ingredients in a processor except hazelnuts. Beat for 2 minutes. Add 1½ C hazelnuts & mix well. Pour into a greased 9x13 pan & sprinkle remaining hazelnuts on top. Bake at 350° for 35 minutes or until top springs back when touched in center. Cool. Serves 12.

desserts and pies

APPLE CUSTARD

5 apples	1 C hot milk
3 T butter	1 T vanilla
¾ t cinnamon	2 T cognac
¾ t nutmeg	⅔ C flour
1 C butter	¼ C brown sugar
¾ C sugar	¼ t salt
6 eggs	evaporated milk

Slice apples & saute in butter with ¼ t of the cinnamon & nutmeg for 10 minutes. Cream ½ C butter & ¾ C sugar. Add eggs & milk & flavorings. Heat gently whisking until smooth & thickened. Arrange apples in a large greased baking dish; pour custard over top. Mix dry ingredients with the remaining spices & cut in remaining butter until coarse crumbs. Sprinkle over custard. Bake at 350° for 45 minutes til bubbly. Serve with milk. Serves 8.

BLUEBERRY GRUNT

4 C blueberries	1½ C flour
½ C sugar	½ t salt
2 t baking powder	¼ t nutmeg
2 t grated orange peel	¾ C milk

Mix blueberries & sugar in a skillet & cook until juices start to boil. Lower heat. Mix dry ingredients & milk & stir just until moistened. Drop dough by spoonfuls on top of simmering blueberries. You should have 8 dumplings. Cover & cook 10-15 minutes until dough is puffed. Serve with thick cream. Serves 8.

"The very smell of mint rejuvenates the spirit"

HEALTHY HASH BROWN PUDDING

12 oz frozen hash browns
½ C brown sugar
½ C molasses
¼ C butter
1 egg
¾ C grated carrot
1 ½ C flour
1 ¼ t salt
1 t cinnamon
½ t nutmeg
¾ t soda
1 C raisins
⅔ C candy fruits
⅔ C walnuts

Thaw & separate hash browns. Cream sugar, molasses & butter. Add egg, carrot & hash browns. Add dry ingredients, beating just until moistened. Chop raisins, candied fruits & walnuts & stir in mixture. Pour into a greased ring mold; cover loosely with foil. Set pan in 1 inch of hot water & bake at 375° for 1 hour & 10 minutes or until it tests done. Let stand 10 minutes then turn out & cool. Heat before serving with Orange Mace Hard Sauce. Serves 8.

ORANGE MACE HARD SAUCE

3 C powdered sugar
¼ C orange juice
¾ C butter
½ t mace
2 t grated orange peel

Combine all ingredients in a processor. Puree until light & fluffy.

CURRIED FRUIT CUP

A quick gourmet dessert to have on hand.

32 oz fruit salad
1 C chopped chutney
1 t nutmeg
1 t curry
1 t grnd ginger
1 T wine vinegar

Drain fruit salad. Mix all other ingredients and serve on top of fruit salad. Broil for 3 minutes until top is bubbly. Serves 6.

desserts and pies

ACAPULCO BANANAS

6 bananas	1 t cinnamon
3 T lemon juice	⅛ t nutmeg
12 flour tortillas	¼ C milk
⅔ C sugar	Chocolate Sauce

Peel bananas & cut in half lengthwise; dip in lemon juice. Place each half on end of tortilla. Mix sugar & spices & sprinkle over bananas, reserving a little for the top. Roll each tortilla & secure with a toothpick. Brush with milk & sprinkle remaining spices over. Place on a greased baking sheet & bake at 400° for 15 minutes. Remove from sheet & serve with Chocolate Sauce. Serves 12.

SAUCE:

8 oz chocolate bar	6 oz milk
pinch of salt	1 t vanilla

Cook all together until thickened. Serve warm.

TEQUILA SUNSET SORBET

3 T sugar	3 T lime juice
3 T boiling water	⅓ C tequila
2½ C orange juice	¼ C grenadine

Combine sugar & water & stir to dissolve. Cover & chill. Add to juices and tequila. Pour into a 9x5 loaf pan & freeze for 8 hours or until firm. Break the frozen mixture into chunks; add grenadine. Put in processor & blend until smooth but not melted. Cover & chill again until firm. Serves 4.

The Egyptians in 1550 put a garlic clove into a woman's womb before bed and if no garlic odor was noted on her breath in the morning she was said to be infertile.

desserts and pies

GEORGIA PEACH SOUFFLE

½ C sugar
1 env unflavored gelatin
¼ t nutmeg
⅛ t salt
½ C water
4 eggs, separated

1 T lemon juice
½ t vanilla
¼ t almond extract
4 peaches
½ C cream

Mix sugar, gelatin, nutmeg & salt & stir in water. Heat until gelatin dissolves. Beat egg yolks until lemon colored & gradually beat in warm gelatin. Return to heat; add lemon juice & cook until thickened. Remove from heat & add extracts. Peel, pit & chop 2 peaches finely & add to gelatin. Chill until slushy. Chop remaining peaches & fold into mixture along with stiffly beaten egg whites & whipped cream. Pour into a souffle dish & chill until firm. Garnish with almonds & mint leaves. Serves 8.

COLD LIQUEUR SOUFFLE

The most elegant herb drink - Benedictine

5 eggs, separated
½ C sugar
¾ C Brandy
⅓ C Sherry
¼ C Benedictine

2 T lemon juice
2 T unfl gelatin
½ C water
2 C cream, whipped

Beat egg yolks until thick & add sugar. Add liqueurs & lemon juice & mix well. Soak gelatin in water & heat until dissolved. Remove from heat; add liqueur mixture. Butter a 2 qt souffle dish & sprinkle with sugar. Beat egg whites until stiff & fold into gelatin mixture with the whipped cream. Pour into dish & chill 4-6 hours. Serves 8.

CHINESE GLASS FRUIT

½ C light corn syrup
¾ C water
2 C sugar
1 T sesame seeds

1 ½ lb plums
2 C strawberries
2 bananas
1 lb grapes

Mix corn syrup, water & sugar in a 2½ qt pan. Cook on high until sugar dissolves, stirring constantly. Boil to 300° on a candy thermometer. Pour syrup in a dish over simmering hot water. Add sesame seeds while keeping temperature at a simmer. Skewer fruit onto bamboo sticks & dip into syrup. Immediately plunge into ice water. Serve immediately. Serves 6.

FLORIDA ORANGE IGLOOS

1 qt vanilla ice cream
3½ oz coconut
6 seedless oranges
1 C orange juice

¾ C sugar
3 whole cloves
1 C water
1½ T cornstarch

3 T brandy

Scoop ice cream into 8 balls & roll in coconut. Freeze until serving time. Peel oranges & separate into sections. Mix juice, sugar, cloves & ¾ C water & bring to a boil & simmer 15 minutes. Remove cloves. Blend cornstarch with remaining ¼ C water & stir into juice mixture. Boil gently for 30 seconds. Add orange segments & brandy & serve over ice cream igloos. Serves 8.

The strewing woman & her maids, carrying baskets lined with satin & filled with herbs, scattered fragrant leaves along the monarch's path from the tower to Westminster.

Jones

desserts and pies

LEMON GINGERBREAD

½ C butter
2 T powdered sugar
1 egg
1 C molasses
1 C boiling water
1 t lemon juice

2¼ C flour
1 t soda
½ t salt
1 t ginger
1 t cinnamon
3 oz lemon Jello

Mix all ingredients except Jello until blended. Beat until smooth. Pour into a greased loaf pan & bake at 325° for 60 minutes. Cool & remove from pan. Slice 1½ inch layer off top of gingerbread & scoop out bottom piece leaving 1½" on bottom & sides. Meanwhile make Jello as package instructs. When half set pour into cavity; replace top & chill until firm. Serves 8.

INDIVIDUAL CHOCOLATE JEWELS

1 C butter
2 C powdered sugar
4 sq unsweet chocolate
1 t peppermint extract

4 eggs
1 t vanilla
pinch of salt
1 C cream

2 C vanilla wafer crumbs

TOPPING:
3 sq unsweet chocolate
1 C powdered sugar

½ C butter
2 eggs

Cream butter & sugar. Melt chocolate & add to butter with peppermint, eggs, vanilla & salt. Mix well. Whip cream until soft peaks form. Fold into mixture. Place 1 t crumbs in bottom of 24 paper lined cupcake tins. Fill with chocolate mixture & sprinkle with remainder of crumbs. For topping, melt chocolate; cream sugar & butter. Add eggs. Spoon a round on each jewel. Freeze. Serve frozen. Makes 24.

MOCHA ALASKA DESSERT

CRUST:
¾ C vanilla wafer crumbs ½ C pecans
¾ C cinnamon graham   ½ C butter
  cracker crumbs   2 T cocoa

Combine all ingredients in a processor. Pat mixture in bottom of a 9" baking pan. Bake at 350° for 8 minutes. Cool.

FILLING:
½ gal coffee ice cream   1 T coffee
6 (1 oz) Heath Bars   liqueur
7 oz marshmallow creme   3 egg whites

Combine ice cream & crumbled candy; spoon on crust. Cover & freeze firm. Mix marshmallow & liqueur until blended. Beat egg whites until foamy & add marshmallow mixture 1 T at a time, beating stiffly. Spread meringue over ice cream, sealing edges. Bake at 475° for 3 minutes. Serves 10.

A NICE SPICE ICE CREAM

1 qt milk   2 T vanilla
2 2" cinnamon sticks   ½ t grn cinnamon
1½ C sugar   ½ t grn nutmeg
1 t salt   ¼ t grn cloves
         1 qt heavy cream

Heat milk & cinnamon sticks to almost boiling & dissolve sugar & salt in the milk. Let cool. Add all else & chill for 2 hours. Remove cinnamon sticks. Freeze in ice cream freezer as stated. Makes 3 qts.

Mix 1 C chopped candied ginger & 2 T rum into 1 qt vanilla ice cream. Beat until light & fluffy. Freeze firm. Serves 8.

LAVENDER & HONEY ICE CREAM

4 C cream
½ C herb honey
5 egg yolks
a few lavender blossoms

Mix together 3 C cream, honey & egg yolks & cook, stirring constantly until mixture thickens, about 10 minutes. Add the blossoms the last minute of cooking. Strain & stir in remaining cup of cream. Cover & chill freeze in ice cream freezer. Serves 8.

LIME MINT SHERBET

16 mint leaves
2 C water
¾ C sugar
½ C corn syrup
½ C lime juice
2 T lime rind
2 egg whites, beaten stiffly

Boil mint, water & sugar for 5 minutes. Cool & strain. Add corn syrup, lime juice & grated rind. Freeze, stirring often. At first stirring, add the stiffly beaten egg whites & freeze firm. Serves 6.

GARDEN MINT ICE CREAM

1½ C sugar
1½ C water
2 C crushed mint leaves
½ C light corn syrup
1 C pineapple juice
1 C chopped pineapple
2 C milk
2 C cream
¼ C mint liqueur

Boil sugar & water until soft ball stage. Add mint leaves & cook 10 minutes. Remove from heat & strain. Stir in corn syrup. Cool. Add pineapple juice & fresh pineapple, milk, cream & mint liqueur. Freeze in ice cream freezer. Makes 2 qts.

desserts and pies

ANGEL'S FOOD WITH AMARETTO SAUCE

⅓ C water
2 T sugar
1½ t cornstarch
2 T Amaretto

½ t lemon juice
1½ T almonds
¼ t almond extract
angel food cake

Mix all ingredients in a pan until blended. Heat until mixture begins to boil & boil 1 minute until mixture is thickened & bubbly. Stir in Amaretto & juice but do not boil. Remove from heat. Slice almonds & stir in with extract. Serve on top of angel food cake slices. Serves 4.

FRUITY GINGERBREAD

1½ C whole wheat flour
½ C white flour
¾ C wheat germ
1½ t soda
1 T grated orange rind
½ C chopped dates
½ C brown sugar
¼ C melted butter

1 t cinnamon
1 t ginger
½ t salt
½ C raisins
1 egg
¼ C molasses
1 C hot water
¾ C honey

Mix all ingredients until blended. Pour into a greased 9 x 13 pan & bake at 350° for 40 - 60 minutes until done. Serve with a flavored yogurt such as coffee.

LEMON BALM CUSTARD

6 egg yolks
6 T sugar

4½ T lemon juice
9 T heavy cream

1 T minced lemon balm leaves

Whisk the yolks, sugar, juice & 3 T cream over low heat until thick. Pour in a bowl & cool. Whip cream to soft peaks form. Fold into custard; chill. Serves 8.

SHERRIED RUM CAKE

This is really an instant dessert, although it is best to assemble it ahead of time to blend the flavors.

½ C sherry
½ C rum
1 pound cake
raspberry jam
1 t mace
1 C cream
½ C mint leaves

Mix the liquors & slowly pour over the cake. Mix the jam and the mace & ice the cake. Whip cream until stiff peaks form. Garnish cake with cream and mint leaves.

ROSEMARY DATE NUT PUDDING

¼ C butter
½ C sugar
1 egg
⅓ C buttermilk
1 C flour
1 T grtd orange peel
2 t rosemary
½ t soda
½ t salt
1 C pitted dates
1 C pecans
2 T sugar
6 T orange liqueur

Cream butter & ½ C sugar. Add egg & buttermilk. Add dry ingredients, beating just until moistened. Stir in chopped dates & nuts. Pour into a greased 1½ qt dish & bake at 350° for 25-30 minutes. Stir liqueur & 2 T sugar together until sugar dissolves. Pour syrup over hot pudding; let stand until syrup is completely absorbed, about 15 minutes. Unmold & garnish with rosemary sprigs & blossoms. Serve warm with whipped cream. Serves 8.

"If Christmas falls on Monday, the winter will be long and cold; but when it falls on a Wednesday, there will be a splendid summer & a beautiful harvest."

desserts and pies

MOCHA MOUSSE PIE

CRUST:
1 ¼ C chocolate wafers	1 T sugar
1 egg white	2 T butter

FILLING:
2 t unflavored gelatin	¼ C sugar
¼ C cold water	½ t almond extr.
1 T cocoa	1 C hot water
1 T instant coffee powder	1 C ricotta

For crust, crush wafers & mix all crust ingredients together & press on bottom & sides of 9" pie plate. Bake at 425° for 5 minutes until golden. For filling, sprinkle gelatin over cold water & let stand. Mix cocoa, coffee powder, sugar & almond extract & add very hot or boiling water & stir until sugar dissolves. Add gelatin. Cool. Combine all ingredients in a processor with the ricotta cheese. Puree until smooth & pour into crust. Chill until set.

COCOA AMARETTO PIE

CRUST:
2 C coconut	2 T butter
6 oz chocolate chips	1 T corn syrup

FILLING:
¼ C amaretto liqueur	1 t cinnamon
2 t unflavored gelatin	1 ½ C cream
1 C powdered sugar	½ C sour cream
¾ C ground almonds	

For crust, warm coconut; melt chocolate & add butter & syrup. Pour chocolate over warm coconut; blend thoroughly. Press mixture on bottom & sides of a 9" pie plate. For filling, combine liqueur with gelatin & heat just until dissolved. Add all else but almonds & whip until stiff. Fold in toasted almonds & pour in shell. Chill.

desserts and pies

BUTTERSCOTCH PEACH PIE

2 9" pie shells
3 lbs sliced peaches
¼ C brown sugar
2 T flour
2 t lemon juice
6 T butter
½ t nutmeg
¼ t almond ext.

Separate 2 pie shells, reserving one for top. Arrange peaches over bottom crust. Add remaining ingredients & sprinkle over peaches. Top with other crust & cut slit for steam to escape. Bake at 350° for 50 minutes until golden. Serve hot or cold.

GOOD & EVIL ICE CREAM PIE

The guilt won't get you with this dessert!

CRUST:

1 C uncooked oats
⅓ C wheat germ
⅓ C brown sugar
½ t cinnamon
¼ C melted butter

FILLING:

¼ C honey
¼ t nutmeg
¾ t cinnamon
⅛ t cloves
½ gal vanilla ice cream

For crust, mix all ingredients until blended. Press mixture on bottom & sides of a 9" pie plate. Bake at 375° for 10 minutes until brown. Cool. For filling add honey & spices to ice cream; spoon into crust & freeze until firm.

CINNAMON CHEESECAKE PIE

1 9" pie shell
16 oz cream cheese
¼ C sugar
1 ½ t cinnamon
⅔ C honey
4 eggs

Thaw pie shell. Mix all ingredients & blend well. Pour into pie shell. Bake at 350° for 70 minutes until set.

desserts and pies

MINCEMEAT FOLDOVERS

1 box pie crust	¼ C sherry
2 C prepared mincemeat	¼ t dried mint
¼ C strong coffee	¼ t rosemary

Butter, cinnamon, sugar

Make pastry as directed; roll out thin & cut into 5" squares. Line muffin tins with squares, letting edges hang over. Mix mincemeat, coffee, sherry, dried mint & dried rosemary & put a spoonful in each tin. Fold over corners of pastry to close. Dot with butter & sprinkle with cinnamon & sugar. Bake at 450° for 30 minutes until done.

SURPRISE THANKSGIVING PIE

1 C mincemeat	1 t cinnamon
1 diced apple	¼ t ginger
3 T sherry	1 T soft butter
1 C sugar	½ t salt
3 beaten eggs	1 t allspice
2 C pumpkin	1 C milk

1 unbaked 9" pie shell

Mix mincemeat, apple & sherry & set aside. Mix remaining ingredients except shell & blend. Place mincemeat mixture in bottom of pie shell. Pour pumpkin mixture on top. Bake at 350° for 45 minutes until firm.

While it is undeniably true that people love a surprise, it is equally true that they are seldom pleased to suddenly & without warning happen upon a series of prunes in what they took to be a normal loin of pork.

Fran Lebowitz

desserts and pies

PUMPKIN PARFAIT PIE

½ C brown sugar
4 t unflavored gelatin
1 t instant coffee powder
½ t ginger
½ t cinnamon
¼ t nutmeg
1 C hot water
2 C vanilla ice cream
1 C pumpkin
1 9" graham cracker crust

Blend sugar, gelatin, coffee powder & spices in a bowl. Add hot to boiling water; stir to dissolve. Add ice cream by the spoonful, stirring until smooth. Add pumpkin. Chill until mixture mounds when spooned & place in crust. Chill until firm.

PUMPKIN GINGER PIE

2 beaten eggs
16 oz pumpkin
¾ C sugar
1 t cinnamon
½ t salt
½ t nutmeg
⅛ t cloves
1⅔ C milk
½ C chopped candied ginger
2 unbaked 9" pie shells

Mix all ingredients until blended. Pour into crusts & bake at 425° for 15 minutes. Turn oven down to 350° & bake for 30 minutes until knife inserted comes clean. Cool. Makes 2 pies.

During the Victorian era, rose petals were frequently used in pies and jams and to scent butter.

"That as many herbs & flowers with their fragrant sweet smells do comfort & as it were revive the spirits & perfume a whole house. Parkinson

desserts and pies

BENEDICTINE PIE

Suppose the monks ever made this delight?

1 ½ C gingersnap crumbs	⅛ t salt
¼ C melted butter	3 eggs, separated
½ C cold water	½ C Benedictine
1 env unflavored gelatin	⅓ C sugar
⅓ C sugar	1 C cream

Combine crumbs & butter. Press mixture on bottom & sides of a 9" pie plate. Bake at 350° for 10 minutes. Cool. Pour water in pan & sprinkle gelatin over. Heat with ⅓ C sugar, salt & egg yolks until gelatin dissolves & mixture thickens. Do not boil. Remove from heat. Stir in Benedictine & chill until mixture mounds slightly.. Beat egg whites until stiff; add remaining sugar & beat until peaks are firm. Fold whites into thickened mixture. Whip cream until soft peaks form. Fold into mixture. Pour into crust. Chill overnight.

HIDDEN SURPRISE APPLE PIE

12 sliced apples	¼ t salt
¾ C sugar	2 9" pie shells
½ C flour	6 T butter
1 t apple pie spice	3 T bourbon
1 t cinnamon	1 C pecan halves
1 t nutmeg	1 C cream

Place sliced apples in large bowl. Add dry ingredients & mix well to coat apples. Place mixture in 1 pie shell. Melt butter; remove from heat & add bourbon. Pour over apples. Cover with pecan halves, then with other pie shell. Make a air hole. Bake at 425° for 50 minutes. When done & while still warm, pour cream through hole in pie. Serve warm.

a pomander of cakes and cookies

The bodily aromas had to be masked
From the eighteenth century home;
Spice studded lemons worn round the neck
Meant you never had to dine alone.

LEMON POUNDCAKE

Make this cake a day ahead for flavor.

8 oz cream cheese	¾ C milk
4 eggs	2 T lemon peel
18 oz yellow cake mix	3 T lemon balm

Beat cream cheese until fluffy. Add eggs one at a time beating well after each. Beat in cake mix alternately with milk, beginning & ending with mix. Grate the peel & chop the lemon balm finely & blend in. Pour into a 9" tube pan & bake at 350° for 55 minutes or until done.

GREEK SPICE CAKE

Could this be why these Greeks are so Adonis like?

1 C oil	1 t soda
1 C brown sugar	1⅓ C buttermilk
2 t almond extract	1 C sugar
1 t baking powder	3 eggs
1 t cinnamon	2½ C flour
1 t cloves	2 t salt
1 t nutmeg	1 C pecans

Mix the oil & brown sugar. Add remaining ingredients with chopped pecans & mix well. Pour into a greased 9x13 pan & bake at 350° for 35 minutes. Cool. Ice with 2 C sugar & ¾ C water heated if desired.

"Sassafras called by ther inhabitants "Winauk", a kind of wood of most pleasant and secret smell and of most rare virtues in physick for the cure of many diseases".

cakes and cookies

INDIAN PECAN POUND CAKE

1½ C flour
½ C yellow cornmeal
½ t salt
2 t baking powder
¾ C soft butter
1½ C sugar
4 eggs
⅓ C milk
¼ C dark rum
2 t cinnamon
¼ C whole pecans

Mix dry ingredients, butter & eggs & beat until light. Add milk slowly with the rum & cinnamon & stir in pecans. Pour into a greased loaf pan & bake at 350° for 60 minutes. Cool.

ORANGE ZUCCHINI POUND CAKE

1 C butter
2 C brown sugar
1 T grated orange peel
1 t cinnamon
½ t nutmeg
¼ t cloves
½ t salt
3 C flour
3 t baking powder
4 eggs
½ C orange juice
1 C zucchini

Cream butter & sugar. Add dry ingredients, beating just until moistened. Add eggs, beating after each addition. Add juice. Grate zucchini & fold in batter. Pour into a greased bundt pan; bake at 350° for 60 minutes. Cool 10 minutes & remove from pan.
Variation: Add ½ C cocoa in place of ½ C flour.

Walpurgis Night comes on April 30. This is the night when witches and warlocks are roaming around up to no good at all. People in ancient days knew when to warn them off. They tied bundles of herbs to poles, set them afire & raced valiantly around their homes defeating the evil spirits at their own games. Give a bundles of tied herbs on April 30 as a "witch chaser".

cakes and cookies

CINNAMON CRUNCH POUND CAKE

18½ oz yellow cake mix	1 T cinnamon
¾ C milk	2 t allspice
½ C molasses	¼ t cloves

Topping:

¾ C brown sugar	½ C butter
⅓ C flour	¼ C milk
2 t cinnamon	½ C walnuts

Prepare cake mix according to package directions, substituting milk & molasses for water & adding spices. Pour into 2 greased loaf pans & bake at 350° for 45 minutes. Cool 10 minutes & remove from pans. Mix topping ingredients with chopped nuts & sprinkle over top of cakes to cover completely & evenly. Broil under broiler with cakes 3" from heat for 2 minutes until bubbly. Watch carefully. Cool.

TIPSY PECAN POUND CAKE

Scarlett may have eaten this cake in Tara's heyday.

1 C butter	1 t salt
2 t baking powder	½ t nutmeg
2½ C sugar	1 C sour cream
6 eggs	½ C + 2 T bourbon
3 C flour	1 C pecan pieces
2 C powder sugar	

Cream butter & sugar until light & fluffy. Add eggs, one at a time, beating after each addition. Mix dry ingredients together & add alternately with sour cream & ½ C bourbon. Fold in chopped pecans. Pour into a greased bundt pan & bake at 350° for 60 minutes. Cool 15 minutes & remove from pan. Make glaze with 2 T bourbon & 2 C powdered sugar adding more bourbon if necessary to make a smooth glaze. Pour over cake.

CHOCOLATE MOUSSE LOG CAKE

1 C heavy cream	¼ C Kahlua
1½ T cocoa	20 choco. wafers
2 T powdered sugar	1 t cocoa
½ t cinnamon	1 t powder.sugar

Whip cream until soft peaks form. Fold in cocoa, 2 T sugar & cinnamon. Add liqueur & beat until stiff. Spread each wafer with 1 T of the mixture. Sandwich the wafers together on their sides in a 12" long dish to form a log. Ice log with remaining whipped cream. Chill overnight. When serving, sprinkle with 1 t cocoa & 1 t powdered sugar. Cut diagonally in slices.

CHOCOLATE PUMPKIN POUND CAKE

1 C butter	2¾ C flour
2 C sugar	¾ C cocoa
4 eggs	1 t soda
2 t vanilla	¼ t salt
12 oz chocolate chips	½ t cinnamon
2 t baking powder	2 C pumpkin

Cream butter & sugar until light & fluffy. Add eggs, one at a time, beating after each addition. Add vanilla. Mix chocolate chips with dry ingredients & add alternately with pumpkin. Pour into a greased bundt pan & bake at 325° for 1 hour 20 minutes or until it tests done. Let cool 5 minutes before removing from pan.

Feed moderately on wholesome foods; garden herbs surpass rich viands.
Old Chinese Proverb

cakes and cookies

CHIFFON BANANA CAKE

2 eggs, separated
1⅓ C sugar
1¾ C flour
1 t soda
1 t baking powder
1 t salt

1 C bananas
⅔ C buttermilk
1 t vanilla
½ C chopped nuts
1 t mace
⅓ C oil

Beat egg yolks. Add sugar & beat well. Add flour, soda, baking powder & salt alternately with bananas & buttermilk. Add vanilla, nuts, mace & oil beating just until mixed. Beat egg whites stiff & fold into mixture. Pour into 2 greased cake pans & bake at 325° for 25 minutes or until cakes test done. Cool & frost if desired.

WINTER'S APPLESAUCE CAKE

½ C oil
1 egg
1 C applesauce
1½ t vanilla
1½ C flour
1 t baking powder
1 C sugar

1 t soda
½ t salt
¾ t cinnamon
½ t allspice
¼ t nutmeg
¼ t cloves
1 C raisins

¾ C chopped walnuts

Cream oil, egg, applesauce & vanilla until light & fluffy. Mix all dry ingredients together & add in three additions. Stir in raisins & nuts. Pour into a greased 9" square pan & bake at 350° for 60 minutes.

Frosting:
1½ C powdered sugar
2 T whipping cream

2 T butter
½ t vanilla

Combine all in a processor. Puree until spreadable. Frost cake when cool.

ROSE GERANIUM CAKE

The Southern cook used rose geranium leaves when vanilla was a casualty of the War Between the States.

1 C butter
3 C sugar
4 eggs
¼ t soda
a grating of nutmeg

3 C flour
⅔ t vanilla
1 C buttermilk
½ C cocoa
16 rose geranium leaves

Cream butter & sugar until light & fluffy. Add eggs, one at a time, beating after each addition. Mix next three ingredients together & add alternately with vanilla & buttermilk & beat smooth. Remove ⅔ C batter from bowl & blend in cocoa. In a greased & floured tube pan place the fresh rose geranium leaves bottom side up after rubbing to release aroma. Cover the bottom. Pour vanilla mixture in pan. Spoon cocoa batter in 5 places & swirl each spoonful. Bake at 350° for 60 minutes & remove from oven. Run knife around edge & remove to cool.

BITTERS AND WALNUT CAKE

5 eggs, separated
6 T sugar

1 C walnuts
¼ C bread crumbs

1 t Angostura aromatic bitters

Combine all ingredients except egg whites in a processor. Beat egg whites until stiff & fold in. Pour into a greased bundt pan & bake at 350° for 60 minutes. Cool.
Make syrup by boiling 1½ C sugar, ½ C water, juice of 1 lemon & 2 T aromatic bitters for 2 minutes. Spoon hot syrup over cake slowly so cake absorbs the syrup. Serve with whipped cream.

ROCKIN ROLLIN JAM CAKE

½ C butter	2 C flour
1 C sugar	2 t cinnamon
4 eggs	1 t allspice
⅔ C buttermilk	1 t soda

12 oz lemon marmalade

Frosting:

⅓ C milk choco. chips	½ C butter
2 C powdered sugar	1 T milk
1 C brown sugar	½ C pecans

Cream butter & sugar until light & fluffy. Add eggs, one at a time with buttermilk. Mix dry ingredients together & stir just until blended. Fold in ½ C jam until swirls of jam are just visible. Do not overmix. Pour into 2 greased pans & bake at 350° for 25 minutes. Cool.

For frosting, melt chocolate chips until smooth. Cool. Combine all ingredients except pecans in a processor. Puree until smooth.

To assemble, place one layer on a plate & spread remaining jam over top & add 2nd layer on top. Frost with chocolate frosting & sprinkle with chopped pecans.

SPICED YOGURT POUND CAKE

1 C butter	2½ C flour
2 C sugar	½ t soda
4 eggs	¼ t salt
1½ t apple pie spice	1 C plain yogurt

Cream butter & sugar. Add eggs. Mix dry ingredients & add with yogurt. Stir until blended. Pour in a greased bundt pan & bake at 350° for 60 minutes. Cool. Make frosting with 1 C plain yogurt, ½ C brown sugar, ½ t apple pie spice. Pour over cake.

CRANBERRY KEEPING CAKE

2½ C cranberries
⅔ C sugar
1 t grated orange rind
½ C butter
2¼ C flour
2 C brown sugar
½ t cardamon
½ t ground coriander

2 t cinnamon
¼ t cloves
¾ t salt
2 eggs
¾ C sour cream
2 t soda
2 t water
1 C pecan pieces

Bring 1½ C cranberries, sugar & rind to a boil & cook until berries have popped. Chop remaining berries & add to berries in pan. Cool. Melt butter until creamy, not melted & set aside. Mix dry ingredients & add to eggs, sour cream, soda & water beating just until mixed. Beat in butter, cranberry mixture & chopped nuts. Pour into 2 greased loaf pans & bake at 350° for 60 minutes. Cool 15 minutes in pan.

COFFEE SPICE CAKE

1 C honey
1 C undiluted orange juice
½ C oil
⅓ C coffee
¾ C sugar
4 eggs
2 t baking powder

3¼ C flour
1 t soda
1 t cinnamon
½ t ginger
½ t allspice
½ t salt
1 C nut pieces

Cream honey, orange juice concentrate, oil, coffee & sugar until light & fluffy. Add eggs. Mix dry ingredients together & add to liquids. Fold in nuts. Pour into 2 greased loaf pans & bake at 350° for 15 minutes then 325° for 45 minutes. Cool.

cakes and cookies

SURPRISINGLY LIKEABLE FRUITCAKE

1 C oil	1 C coconut
3 eggs	1 C candy cherries
2 t vanilla	2 C flour
1½ C cooked carrots	2 C sugar
¾ C drained pineapple	2 t soda
1 C chopped walnuts	2 t cinnamon
¼ C brandy	

Mix the oil, eggs & vanilla. Fold in the pureed carrots, crushed pineapple, nuts, coconut, halved cherries with the dry ingredients & mix well. Pour into a greased 9 x 13 pan & bake at 350° for 60 minutes until edges pull away from pan. Prick cake with a cake tester & pour ½ the brandy on top slowly allowing to soak in. Cool 15 minutes & remove from pan. Prick rest of cake & pour remaining brandy over.

STRAWBERRY CRUNCH CAKE

20 oz thawed strawberries	½ t salt
1 C butter	1 t cinnamon
1¼ C sugar	½ t soda
2 eggs	2 C flour
1 C sour cream	½ C walnuts
1 t baking powder	½ C brown sugar

Drain strawberries, reserving syrup. Cream butter & sugar until light & fluffy. Add eggs & sour cream. Mix dry ingredients together & add to creamed mixture. Pour half the mixture into a greased 9x13 pan & spoon the drained strawberries on top of batter. Combine chopped walnuts & brown sugar & sprinkle half of this on berries. Repeat with batter & walnuts & bake at 350° for 40 minutes. Serve with reserve syrup if desired.

PUMPKIN BROWNIES

½ C butter
2 C brown sugar
1 C pumpkin
2 eggs
1 t vanilla
2 t pumpkin pie spice
1 t baking powder

1½ C flour
1½ C oats
½ t soda
½ t salt
½ C walnuts
2 C butterscotch bits
½ C semi-sweet chocolate bits

Cream butter & sugar until light & fluffy. Add pumpkin, eggs & vanilla. Mix in dry ingredients & chopped walnuts. Pour into a greased jelly roll pan & bake at 350° for 25 minutes. Immediately sprinkle on butterscotch morsels; let stand 5 minutes & spread to cover brownies. Melt chocolate chips & drizzle over top like a spider web. Yields 3 dozen.

CHOCOLATE CRANBERRY BARS

4 oz chocolate
1 C butter
1½ C sugar
2 eggs
1 C whole cranberry sauce
1 t vanilla

2 C flour
½ t soda
¾ t ginger
¾ t cinnamon
½ t cloves
½ C buttermilk

Melt chocolate & cool. Cream butter & sugar until light & fluffy. Add eggs, one at a time, beating after each addition. Add whole berry cranberry sauce, vanilla & chocolate. Mix dry ingredients together & add alternately with milk. Pour into a greased 9x13 pan & bake at 350° for 40 minutes. Cool 10 minutes & remove from pan. Yields 30 bars.

cakes and cookies

PEANUT BUTTER BANANA SQUARES

⅓ C peanut butter
1 chopped banana
½ t baking powder
¼ t salt
2 eggs
¾ C flour
½ t cinnamon
2 T honey
1 t vanilla
2 t oil

Combine all ingredients in a processor. Puree until just mixed. Pour into a greased 8" square pan & bake at 350° for 15 minutes. Cool & cut into squares. Makes 16 squares.

CARAMEL NUT BARS

14 oz caramels
½ C evaporated milk
18.5 oz German Chocolate Cake mix
1 t cinnamon
½ t ginger
½ C butter
1 C semi-sweet chocolate chips
1½ C walnuts

Melt caramels with ⅓ C milk, stirring until smooth & set aside. Mix remaining milk & cake mix, spices & melted butter & press half of mixture in the bottom of a 9x13 pan. Bake at 350° for 8 minutes. Sprinkle with chocolate chips & 1 C chopped walnuts; top with caramel mixture & spread to edge of pan. Top with spoonfuls of remaining cake mixture; press gently into caramel mixture. Sprinkle with remaining nuts. Bake 16 minutes. Cool & cut into bars. Yields 2 dozen.

Old people shouldn't eat health foods. They need all the preservatives they can get.
            Robert Orben

MINT MELTAWAYS

1 C butter
1 C crushed butter mints
2 C flour
1 T sugar

Cream butter until light & add mints & flour. Blend well. Chill dough 1 hour & roll thin. Sprinkle with sugar. Cut in 1½" squares. Bake at 325° for 15 minutes until light golden. Yields 3 dozen.

VERMONT'S OATMEAL COOKIES

¾ C butter
1 C sugar
2 eggs
2 C oats
1 C chopped raisins
2 t pumpkin pie spice
2 C flour
1 t salt
1 t soda
½ C milk
2 T maple flavor
1 C pecan pieces

Cream butter & sugar until light & fluffy. Add eggs, oats & raisins. Mix dry ingredients together & add alternately with milk & maple flavor. Stir in pecans. Drop by spoonfuls on a greased baking sheet. Bake at 350° for 15 minutes. Yields 6 dozen.

HERB SEED COOKIES

½ C butter
½ C sugar
½ C molasses
1 egg
2½ C flour
2 T ginger
1 T coriander seeds
1 t cloves
1 t cinnamon
¼ t salt
½ t soda
6 T hot water
2 T anise seeds
1 T sesame seeds

Blend all ingredients in a processor. Drop by spoonfuls on a baking sheet. Bake at 350° for 8 minutes. Yields 4 dozen.

cakes and cookies

PUMPKIN NUT MACAROONS

⅔ C honey
½ C pumpkin
¼ t crushed anise seeds
4 C coconut
¼ C pistachios
4 egg whites
½ C chopped pumpkin seeds

Mix all ingredients with stiffly beaten egg whites until blended. Add more coconut if batter is too thin. Drop by spoonfuls on a greased baking sheet. Bake at 300° for 25-30 minutes until golden brown. Let cookies stand 10-15 minutes before removing from sheet. They will be soft. When oven has cooled to 150° return to oven & leave overnight. Yields 3 dozen.

LEMON CLOVE COOKIES

½ lb butter
¾ C sugar
1 t vanilla
1 T orange peel
1 egg
pinch of salt
2⅓ C flour
¼ t cloves

Cream butter & sugar until light & fluffy. Add vanilla & peel & egg. Mix dry ingredients together & add to mixture. Roll in 2 logs, wrap & chill for at least 2 hours. Slice dough ¼" thick & place on a baking sheet ½" apart. Bake at 350° for 8-10 minutes until pale golden. Yields 54.

APPLE ENGLISH MUFFIN PASTRIES

4 split English muffins
3 sliced apples
2 oz cream cheese
2 T sugar
¼ t allspice
2 T butter

Layer muffins with apples & cream cheese. Sprinkle rest of ingredients over top. Broil 6-8 minutes. Makes 6.

cakes and cookies

LEMON CRISPERS

¾ C butter 2 C flour
1 C sugar ¾ C soda
7½ oz inst lemon pudd mix pinch salt
3 eggs ½ t mint

Combine all ingredients in a processor. Puree until smooth. Drop by spoonfuls on a greased baking sheet. Bake at 375° for 8-10 minutes. Yields 72.

GINGER ROUNDS

¾ C butter 2½ C flour
1 C brown sugar 2 t soda
1 egg ½ t cloves
4 T molasses 1 t cinnamon
¼ t salt 1¼ t ginger

Combine all ingredients in a processor. Drop by spoonfuls 2" apart on a baking sheet. Flatten with a wet fork dipped in sugar & sprinkle with a drop of water on each. Bake at 350° for 15 minutes. Yields 5 dozen.

QUAKER CRACKERS

½ C butter (only) 1 egg
¼ C sugar 1 t vanilla
1 T brown sugar ¾ C flour
48 slivers candied ginger

Combine all ingredients except candied ginger in a processor. Drop by half spoonfuls 2" apart on a baking sheet. Center on each a thin sliver of candied ginger. Bake at 350° for 6-8 minutes. Remove to rack to cool at once. Yields 3 dozen.

PEANUT BUTTER STICKS

12 slices raisin bread, toasted lightly
1 oz chopped unsalted peanuts
1 T cinnamon
½ C + 2 T peanut butter

Cut crusts from bread & cut in half. Put crusts & any leftover raisins in processor. Process to make coarse crumbs. Mix crumbs, peanuts & cinnamon. Melt peanut butter on low until smooth. Cool slightly. With fork, dip bread in peanut butter, coating well, then press into crumbs to coat. Dry for 1 hour. Makes 24.

ANISE & SESAME SEED COOKIES

1 C olive oil
1 2" strip lemon peel
2 t anise seeds
2 t sesame seeds
1 t orange rind
1 t lemon rind
⅓ C sugar
½ C white wine
2¼ C flour
1 T cinnamon
¼ C sliced almonds

Heat olive oil & add lemon peel & seeds. Remove from heat & cool to room temperature. Remove the peel & add the oil & seeds together with the grated rinds, sugar & wine. Add flour & cinnamon & stir well. Let dough rest for 30 minutes. Divide dough into 12 flat cookies on a baking sheet. Place the almond slices on each. Bake at 400° for 40 minutes until firm to the touch. Makes 12.

When herb bouquets were sent rather than given, the maiden carefully studied the position of the knot in the ribbon. Tied from the right or left it intoned the feelings of the giver or receiver.

PUMPKIN FUDGE

2 C sugar
2 T light corn syrup
1 T pumpkin
⅓ C condensed milk
¼ t pumpkin pie spice

⅓ C milk
2 T butter
½ t vanilla
pinch of salt
food coloring

Combine first 6 ingredients in a pan & cook over medium heat until it boils. Stir constantly. Reduce heat & cook until it reaches soft ball stage. Remove from heat & cool slightly. Add the butter & stir until melted. Add vanilla & salt & orange food color if needed. Beat with a wooden spoon until thick & creamy & holds shape. Pour into a 9x5 pan & cool. Makes 28.

SESAME CRUNCH CANDY

½ C chunky peanut butter
1¾ C cornflakes

½ C honey
1 C sesame seeds

Mix peanut butter, cornflakes & honey until blended. Chill 15 minutes. Toast sesame seeds in small skillet & place in flat bowl. Roll peanut butter mixture in small balls & roll in seeds to coat well. Store in refrigerator. Makes 40.

CHEESECAKE TRUFFLES
Two delectable dishes in one recipe!

8 oz cream cheese
1⅓ C graham cracker crumbs
⅔ C chopped walnuts

2 T sugar
1½ t cinnamon
1 t vanilla

Combine all ingredients but ⅓ C crumbs in a processor. Mix well. Shape into 1" balls & roll in remaining crumbs. Cover & chill. Yields 3 dozen.

HERBED NUTS

¼ C butter	⅛ t nutmeg
1½ t pepper	1 t salt
½ t cumin	2 C cashews

ROSY MARY'S ROSEMARY WALNUTS

6 T butter	1 T salt
1 T crumbled rosemary	½ t cayenne
4 C walnuts	

INDIAN CASHEWS

3 T butter	¾ t cumin
1 t curry powder	1 t salt
2 C raw cashews	

SPICED PEANUTS

2 t chili powder	½ t paprika
½ t cumin	¼ t pepper
½ t oregano	3 C peanuts

Place all ingredients in a jelly roll pan & toss to coat nuts evenly. Bake at 375° for 10-12 minutes. Stir often. Serve warm or room temperature. Store in airtight container.

MINTED PECANS

2 C sugar	1 T butter
dash of salt	2 t mint extract
¾ C evaporated milk	4 C pecan halves

Heat sugar, salt, milk & butter over low heat stirring constantly until sugar is dissolved. Cook to soft ball stage. Remove from heat & stir in extract & pecans. Stir to coat well. Turn out on wax paper & separate nuts with a fork. Store airtight.

Variation: Substitute 1 t cinnamon, ½ t cloves, 1 T grated orange rind & 1 T minced citron for the butter & extract.

Herbal Helps

* All herbs are written as for fresh herbs unless stated otherwise. If using dried, use ¼ less.

* Pesto is found on page 10 and Italian Seasoning is found on page 12.

* Oil or margarine may be substituted for butter unless the recipe specifically states to use butter. Salt & pepper are used sparingly so taste for actual seasoning.

* For we modern folk who are looking for our Scarborough Fair magic, the use of herbs can be daunting. Comparing it to ladies clothes helps remember the recipe outfit.

Thyme is a suit - just right for any occasion, to dress up or down.

Rosemary is the basic black dress - always sensational.

Marjoram is chiffon for our lighter moods.

Tarragon is the strapless evening gown, star of the occasion, needing no support & dominating the picture.

Basils are the blouses, suitable for anything & interchangable.

Sage is the sweater & skirt.

Savory is tweed.

Horseradish is the mini skirt - just right on some dishes but on others...

Abbreviations:

T = Tablespoon
t = teaspoon
C = cup

grt = grated
grn = ground
bx = box
choc = chocolate

To dry fresh herbs in microwave, spread leaves between two paper towels microwave 2-3 minutes or until dry to the touch.

Other books by Strawberry Patchworks:

Strawberry Patchwork
Strawberry Sportcake
Pumpkin Corner
Sugarplum Visions
Cupids Cuisine

Write Strawberry Patchworks for prices.

To order Parsley, Sage, Rosemary and Mine or any other book by Strawberry Patchworks, send inquiry to:

Strawberry Patchworks
11597 Southington Lane
Herndon, Virginia 22070